ROBERT MARSD[

A Detective Police Officer

of Victorian Liverpool

By Isla Broadwell

For Elizabeth, Harriet, Maria, Florence and Irene.

With thanks to Susan and Wendy.

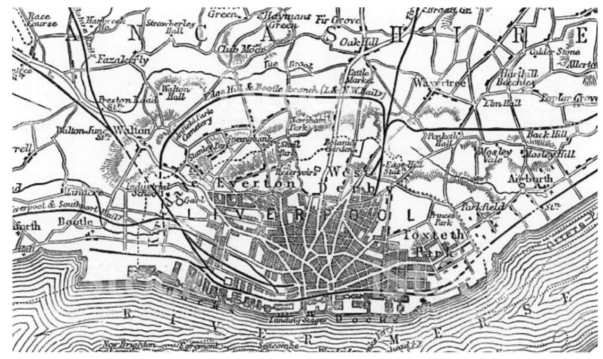

Map of Liverpool. c1860

Liverpool Salthouse Dock by John Atkinson Grimshaw (c1878)

On the steps of the old Liverpool Custom House, late nineteenth century.

William Henry Street, Liverpool (late nineteenth century). Source: www.liverpoolcitypolice

CONTENTS

PROLOGUE

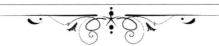

Almond Street had been enveloped in a dense grey fog since early morning. All day its vapour had been rolling uphill from the river, obscuring the port and town of Liverpool in an eerie mantle. As evening closed in however, it had begun to thin and from the window of their butcher's shop, Eliza Hughes was relieved to see that only a ghostly mist remained. A dog's howl, unsettling and desolate, suddenly pierced the silence of the street. "I hope that bloody thing won't be bawling all night," Eliza muttered in irritation. The wail was repeated but this time it seemed closer. Slowly the howl turned into a very human scream.

"Help! Help!"

The metallic clatter of hobnailed boots pounding up the pavement outside drew Eliza to the window. She expected to see the usual night-time scuffle between warring patrons of the public house on the corner of Falkner Street close by. However, as the seconds ticked on, she watched frowning and bewildered as the mist began to increasingly brighten and glow as if a lantern were being carried within it.

The frantic screams and cries for help were right outside now. For a brief second, the vapour became a shining halo as a human figure hurtled past the shop window; its head, hair and arms blazing with fire. As it ran, flames trailed behind it in orange and blue streamers. Wide-eyed with shock and disbelief Eliza ran to the door and looked out. The appalling human torch could still be seen, shimmering as it ran into the gloom. It reached the corner of Lonsdale Street and began to stagger blindly along the pavement; its steps were growing weaker as the flames spread down its torso. The figure sank to its knees and let out a last feeble wail before it slumped forward and with awful finality, fell onto its face.

INTRODUCTION

Robert Marsden was a detective officer in the Liverpool City Police Force during the middle decades of the nineteenth century. The policing of Liverpool was still in its infancy when he joined in the 1850s, and the crimes he investigated reflect the harshness and vulnerability of life in this rapidly growing seaport. Victorian Liverpool was a place where extreme wealth lived cheek-by-jowl with starving poverty. Crime and policing in such a setting was equally basic and unforgiving. This is a biography of Detective Marsden's life as it is told through the contemporary newspaper reports and official police documents in which he appears. To set these in context, maps, illustrations and photographs have been added in an attempt to visualise the Liverpool he saw every day, the people he moved amongst, the streets he walked and the places he worked. Although no picture or photograph of Robert Marsden is known to exist, hundreds of pictures survive of the Liverpool he knew. These give a compelling glimpse of the town and seaport which made up his life and work. Marsden's story reflects the human and social environment of Liverpool when it was at the height of its commercial success.

Robert Marsden is also my great, great, great grandfather.

Finding Detective Robert Marsden

I first learned about Robert Marsden from my maternal grandmother Florence. She told me that her great grandfather was 'one of the first police detectives in Liverpool'. She could tell me nothing else about him; and it was only the chance discovery of a newspaper report from 1866 which gave me any hint that further discoveries about him were possible.

> The Greenock Daily Telegraph
> September 7th 1866
> "ARRIVAL OF READ, THE WIFE MURDERER, FROM AMERICA.- Liverpool, Thursday. – Among the passengers by the steamship City of London, which arrived in Liverpool yesterday from New York, whence she sailed on the 25th ult, was Robert Read or Reid, charged with the murder of his wife in Liverpool in December 1682 [1862]. He was in custody of Marsden, a detective police officer, and on his arrival a large assemblage of "roughs" were in attendance at the landing stage. The prisoner was at once conveyed to Bridewell, and in the course of the day he was brought before Mr Raffles, and at his own desire was remanded for a week. The proceedings were altogether of a formal character, none of the details being entered upon. Read is a slender man, apparently about 35 years of age. Read is stated to have been morose and sulky during the voyage, refusing food for several days."

The report describes a 'detective police officer Marsden' returning to Liverpool from a voyage to New York, escorting a captured wife murderer back to the city in order to face justice. It gives a compelling picture of the murderer, Robert Reid during the journey, describing his morose and sullen behaviour on board ship and the crowd of "roughs" waiting to meet him at Liverpool's Princes Landing Stage (whether to welcome or harangue the prisoner is unclear). It isn't difficult to imagine Detective Marsden's thoughts as he escorted Reid through the rough crowd at the docks, up into the chaotic streets of Liverpool and into the main Bridewell at Cheapside.

I began to research Robert Marsden further and eventually located over four hundred newspaper articles in which he is named and featured. It is a selection of these which form the structure of this book. The *Liverpool Daily Post, Liverpool Mercury* and the satirical periodical *The Porcupine* were the most prolific sources of information. Together they provide fascinating descriptions of the crimes and criminals who were captured by Marsden and brought before the Liverpool Central Police Court on Dale Street. They describe scenes in the courtroom, the behaviour of witnesses and the antics of spectators in the public gallery. In some reports, Detective Marsden is quoted verbatim as he gives evidence during prosecutions.

Featured cases are at times comical, in other instances they are shocking in their brutality or tragic in the picture of poverty and desperation they portray. Language used by journalists is often unforgiving. It shows both a marked lack of empathy for the plight of those whose very poverty forces them into crime and provides an insight into the mindset and values of the Victorian readership. Emphasis is placed on the prisoner's class, facial features, clothing, demeanour and above all their appearance of 'respectability'. These characteristics seem to be the pre-determining factor as to a prisoner's guilt or innocence.

There are many books and narratives written both on the history of Liverpool and on Victorian detectives. In this book I have tried to capture and combine both of these subjects through the real-life experiences of one person, during one decade. Romanticised accounts of Victorian sleuths such as Sherlock Holmes pitted against the machinations of the archetypal criminal genius shape our view of the nineteenth century detective. However, the reality of police detective work in mid-Victorian Liverpool was a far cry from this – it was far less sophisticated and basic.

The Setting
The area covered by the Liverpool City Police force was divided between north and south Liverpool (known as the North and South Divisions). Robert Marsden worked in the North Division which included the notorious wards of North and South Scotland (Road), Netherfield, St Anne's and Vauxhall. These areas contained infamous streets such as Scotland Road, Ben Jonson Street, Richmond Row, Chisenhale Street and Banastrae Street - where, it was said, people lived "more like savages than human beings." Living conditions for the poor and working classes at the time were appalling and the town gained a "notorious reputation for its squalid, overcrowded and damp cellars, where entire families nestled underground in the dark." (Archer, 2011)

Court off Prince Edwin Street. The lower walls were painted with lime whitewash for disinfection and to reflect light back into dark interiors ©Liverpool Records Office, Liverpool Libraries.

By the 1840s the North Division of Liverpool contained a dense system of slum housing known as 'courts'. These were enclosed streets, each containing about ten houses, built around a 'court' yard. In each house there were six to eight rooms and in each of these rooms an entire family (of perhaps eight to ten people) would live, eat and sleep. In the North Division alone there were 2,400 courts which housed a population of about 86,000 people. Added to this were 7,800 cellars into which 39,000 people were also crammed (Macilwee, 2011). Each court possessed one water supply (usually a hand pump) and two toilets. Toilets were basically ashpits which householders were expected to periodically empty themselves. A gutter ran down the middle of each court in which rainwater, rubbish and sewerage would collect.

Unsurprisingly outbreaks of diseases associated with poor sanitation such as cholera and typhoid were common. Charles Dickens, who for the purposes of research, became a 'special constable' in the Liverpool City Police in 1860, saw these poorer areas of Liverpool during a night patrol with North Division police officers. He describes entering a "labyrinth of dismal courts and blind alleys, called 'entries'… attained by noisome passages so profoundly dark that we felt our way with our hands." The North Division also contained many of the city's 1145 pubs, 896 beer houses and 714 brothels.

As a police constable and then a detective in the North Division, Robert Marsden investigated crimes which were most often generated by hunger, poverty and desperation. Theft, shoplifting and alcohol-related violence were the most common crimes. Next were those offences perpetrated by Liverpool's 25,000 street children, by organised gangs, 'roughs', opportunistic criminals and unemployed 'cornermen'. These included larceny, delinquency, deception, embezzlement, assault, battery, manslaughter and murder.

Liverpool had always been a tough place. In 1863, Hughes (a local historian) said that Liverpool was a 'very cruel town' and that "the effects of privateering and the slave trade were still visible in the lower classes and in society in general". Clarkson (1839) explains how sailors working in the "barbarous system of slavery developed savage habits gradually formed by a familiarity with miserable sights.... creating moroseness and cruelty which would brutalize their nature." Even after the abolition of the slave trade, a ruthless culture remained amongst ships' crews and many members of the resident population. The statistics for violent crime in Liverpool between 1863 and 1869 alone record ninety convictions for murder and one hundred and forty one convictions for manslaughter (Archer, 2011). Stabbings and assaults occurred on a daily basis. For example, on 21st September 1860 the *Morning Chronical* reported that: "in Liverpool in the past week there had been at least seven stabbings, three of which were likely to prove fatal… Liverpool can scarcely be surpassed by London, [which has] a population eight times as great."

In addition, sectarian violence between Irish Catholic and Protestant immigrants would boil over into riots and running street battles during the Orange 'marching season' and St Patrick's Day processions. Feuds which began between rival families, villages and counties in Ireland would continue to be fought in the courts and alleys of Liverpool's Vauxhall and Scotland Road districts.

Court off Hornby Street © Liverpool Records Office, Liverpool Libraries.

Crews and passengers from ships arriving in their thousands at Liverpool's docks and landing stages each day also generated their own type of crimes. Newly arrived immigrants were defrauded by 'sharpers' and swindlers offering cut-price (but bogus) berths on board packet steamers to America, Canada and Australia. Meanwhile, thousands of sailors, newly paid after months at sea, would pour into the city's public houses, boarding houses and brothels each day. They included:

> *"Down East Yankees in stovepipe hats chewing long cigars, men from Africa and the West Indies, red-faced bearded Greenland men from the Arctic whaling ships, predatory slavers yellow with fever, stout Prussian traders and seamen from every port in the British Isles, as well as passengers from the packet ships and the truculent, violent packet rats who manned them."*

Evenings of carousing would often end in drunken affray, robbery and prison. Then, as now, alcohol was well known to fuel violence, and street brawls between gangs of sailors and the people of the town were common. Pickpocketing and muggings were frequent as 'cornermen' and criminal gangs worked the docks aiming to relieve naïve passengers and inebriated seamen of their wages, valuables and even clothing. Amongst Liverpool's resident population, domestic violence (often instigated by alcohol) and a culture where inter-marital and family violence was all-pervasive and even accepted; cases of assault, manslaughter and murder formed part of police work. As a detective, Robert Marsden's time policing one of the most violent and crime-ridden districts of a town which was described as 'the most immoral of all immoral places' would have been one of watchful waiting interspersed with moments of random savagery. In a city and at a time when almost every man carried a knife, the work of a Liverpool City Police detective was not for the faint-hearted.

Liverpool Custom House and Salthouse Dock c1865

Robert Marsden was born in Manchester, Lancashire in 1828. Nothing is known of the first twenty-one years of his life, but at some time in the 1840s, he made the thirty-mile journey from his hometown to the thriving port of Liverpool. His exact birth date, place of birth and the names of his parents are not known. Similarly, the date and location of his marriage to his wife Elizabeth Atkinson, a native of Penrith in Cumberland, are also unknown. Exhaustive searches of registry records reveal a frustrating lack of documentation. However, as many genealogists will verify, this is not uncommon. Before 1837, when the official registration of births, deaths and marriages became a matter of law in the British Isles, the recording of these milestones in a person's life was often haphazard. The keeping of accurate and legible records was more or less left to the church; which in turn relied on the tenacity of the parish priest or clerk in updating and storing church registers of baptism, marriage and burial.

The first real record we have of Robert's existence is found in the 1851 census of England and Wales. In this he is aged 22, his new wife Elizabeth is 21 and their daughter Elizabeth (known as Ann) is a year old. The Marsden family were listed as 'visitors' to the Farals who were immigrant Irish dock labourers living in Townsend Street, Everton. Everton at that time was a small village on the hill above Liverpool (known as Everton Brow). Robert's occupation on the census is recorded as 'bookkeeper'. As a bookkeeper Robert's education would have been above average for his time. In 1851, most working people were illiterate (as shown on many marriage certificates where newly-weds often signed their names with a simple 'x'). Therefore, the ability to read, write and calculate with enough proficiency to become a bookkeeper demonstrates that Robert's family must have had some means to pay for his education.

Everton Village c1850 (by Liverpool artist William Gawain Herdman).

Everton appears to have appealed to Robert and his wife Elizabeth. By 1861 they are living in their own house at 16 Gordon Street, with a growing family of six children; Elizabeth Ann (aged 11), Edward (9), William (6), Robert (5), George (3) and Harriet (1). From their home in Everton, the Marsdens had a spectacular view across to the port of Liverpool. Beyond this they could see the River Mersey, the Wirral and the distant Clwydian mountains in Wales.

View of the town and port of Liverpool from Everton Brow in the late 18th century by Liverpool artist William Gawain Herdman.

View of the city of Liverpool taken from the same place in 2020.

View of north Liverpool from Everton Brow, late nineteenth century.

View taken from the same place, 2020.

In the 1850s and 1860s Liverpool was at the height of its commercial success as a cargo and passenger port. At this time, the docklands and river were filled with bristling ships' masts and the smoking funnels of transatlantic steamers. The riverside would have been crammed with dock buildings, landing stages, wharfs, factories, chimneys, and warehouses. As cargo was unloaded, on-shore breezes would carry the scents of their exotic contents across the town and up to Everton's inhabitants on the hill above. Coffee from Brazil, sugar from the West Indies, tobacco from the United States and spices from India, Ceylon and Siam.

With its elevated and healthier position above the town, Everton was considered to be a more attractive place to live. It was known as 'the Montpellier of the county' with large mansion houses, cottages, pleasant gardens, fields, trees and commanding views. It was for this reason that the merchants and ship owners of Liverpool began to build their homes here during the eighteenth century. Many had made fortunes from the African slave trade and from importing goods from all over the world. Liverpool was the main port through which the drivers of Britain's industrial revolution flowed. Cotton, sugar, molasses, silk, spices, rubber, wood, tobacco, petroleum, wheat, tallow, palm oil, brandy, rum, tea and coffee all arrived through Liverpool. By the time Robert Marsden and his family were living there, it was the second port of the British empire and housed the largest population of millionaires per head of population outside of London.

'At Close of Day' by Robert Dudley (1860). The massive scale of Liverpool's commercial success is illustrated in this painting of Canada Dock. Here ships from north America are lined up to unload timber from Canada. Picture courtesy of Liverpool Museums.

Ships moored at Canning Dock on the Strand c1860. The building with columns is Liverpool's old Custom House (destroyed in WWII).

Hundreds of ships moored at Liverpool docks, others are anchored in the river waiting for their turn to dock. An early photograph c1865

The 1850s saw a concerted drive on behalf of national government and city officials to control the levels of crime which had grown as Liverpool's population increased. In the first half of the nineteenth century Liverpool's population had grown from 82,430 in 1801 to 250,000 in 1841. This was mostly due to the mass immigration of Britain's Irish subjects fleeing the potato famine of the 1840s. In 1841 alone 300,000 starving Irish men, women and children arrived in the port. Most immigrants arrived in Liverpool with the intention of travelling on to the United States, Canada and Australia; but many also stayed and made a home in the town.

Liverpool's burgeoning immigrant population was also increased by thousands arriving from other parts of the British Isles and its empire. All came in the hope of benefitting from the wealth and work pouring into the town. Most hoped to settle and make a living in the docks and its ancillary industries of ship building, manufacturing and warehousing.

Starving Irish families fleeing the potato famine. Hundreds of thousands arrived in Liverpool in the 1840s and 1850s

For all newcomers to the town, the immediate securing of employment was crucial; destitution, starvation and the prospect of the workhouse rapidly became a reality for those without work. Even if those who were newly arrived did manage to find employment and a home (or at least access to help from the 'parish') their situation was still precarious. A stark illustration of this can be found in an article in the *Liverpool Mercury* from 1847 in which the death from starvation of eight year-old Irish immigrant, Luke Brothers, is reported. It details that:

> *"since their arrival from Ireland, the Brothers family had lived in a wretched hole in Banastrae Street. The parents and their four or five children were allowed three shillings a week from the parish...whenever the sickly and starving children were well enough to crawl out of their room, they begged from door to door. In the same room as the dead boy were five others lying on a mud floor suffering from typhus."*

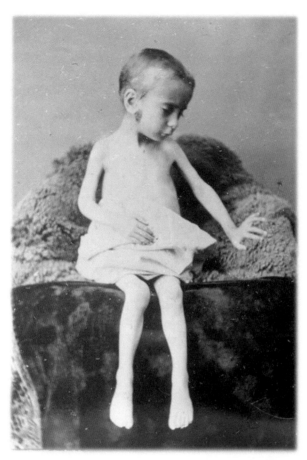

For many destitute families the only viable and legal option would have been admission to the workhouse. The prospect of the workhouse was truly awful for many Victorians. In these establishments, families were forcibly separated into male, female and children's quarters, with no contact allowed between each segregated group. The regime of long hours of hard physical labour and a spartan diet could quickly reduce an inmate to physical and mental ruin. For people desperate to avoid the workhouse, the slippery slope towards crime as a means of basic survival became too great a force to be resisted. Stealing food, money and any article which could be worn, sold or pawned became a way of life for thousands of people.

A child suffering from malnutrition in Liverpool, mid-nineteenth century (Source: Liverpool Records Office, Liverpool Libraries)

'Applicants for Admission to the Casual Ward' (1874) by Liverpool artist Sir Luke Fildes. Destitute families and paupers are pictured waiting in the snow outside of a police station. The police officer on the left is giving out tickets which allows admission to the workhouse for one night.

Bostock Street off Scotland Road. Source: ©Liverpool Records Office, Liverpool Libraries.

In addition to crime being generated by poverty and desperation, authorities in Liverpool were faced with the challenge of policing the thousands of sailors disembarking from vessels docking at the port each day. Intoxication and street brawls between seamen and local residents were a regular night-time occurrence and had been for many years. Hugh Shimmin, a journalist writing in the 1860s, claimed there was a well-known saying in Liverpool that levels of crime in the city were dependent on the direction of the wind. This may seem an outlandish statement at first, but as he points out:

> *"An easterly wind prevailing for a week will carry off from 10,000 to 15,000 seamen; a westerly wind will in a day or two case that number, with replenished pockets, again upon our shore; and the Bridewells, which had been doing slack 'business', speedily become filled again."*

In essence, a westerly wind prevented ships (which relied on an easterly wind to propel them out to sea) from leaving port. If the wind was blowing inland, ships could be stuck in the docks and river for days or even weeks. This left their stranded crews with nothing to do but disembark and go back into the town for further carousing. The number of deaths amongst ships' crews due to knife crime became so frequent that in 1863 Liverpool City Police were forced to act. Handbills, written in seven different languages, were handed out to sailors as they disembarked and were posted in boarding houses, warning against the dangers of carrying of knives.

Sailors Carousing by G. Cruikshank c1850

Sailors in 1850. Thousands of every different nationality could be seen on the streets of Liverpool each day. They walked with a peculiar 'rolling gait' which was the result of spending months on the pitching and heaving decks of sailing vessels.

"The returning crews of the Liverpool privateers were a brutish and anarchic bunch, responsible for many riotous incidents around the dockside districts. The inns and 'slop' clothes-sellers' shops in Pool Lane [now South Castle Street] would be heaving with sailors eager to squander their hard-earned prize money." (Macilwee, 2011)

Castle Street 1860. This is one of the earliest photographs to be taken in Liverpool.

Early Law Enforcement

Before the establishment of the Liverpool City Police in 1836, the town had relied on three different groups of law enforcers to keep order. These were the Corporation constables, the Dock Watch and the town night-watchmen. All three were independent of each other and consisted of men who were undisciplined, badly organised, physically unfit and often drunk. The three groups repeatedly obstructed and fought each other.

The Dock Watch were particularly notorious. Their role was to discourage theft from dock wharves and warehouses, to break-up brawls between sailors and to rescue people who fell or jumped into the river. However, complaints were made that they regularly bullied townspeople, attacked town Corporation constables and locked night-watchmen overnight in their dockside gaols without provocation. Corporation constables (generally known as the 'Day-watch') were seen as even more incompetent. They worked only during regular daytime working hours. They were seen as a highly corrupt body of men who were not averse to taking bribes from criminals in exchange for their silence. They were also often accused of being drunk on duty or simply deserting their posts.

The final group, the town night-watchmen, were of course meant to police the city at night. Known as 'Charlies' their role was to walk through the streets throughout the night, calling out the hour with the famous addendum of "and all is well" (pictured). Their other purposes were to raise the alarm in the event of a fire, apprehend criminals and 'assist' drunks and troublemakers to the local lockup. The night-watchmen came under the authority of the 'Commissioners of Watch, Scavengers and Lamps' and were instructed to "apprehend all night-walkers, rogues, vagabonds and other disorderly persons, disturbing the public". A night-watchman would typically carry a lantern, a long stick or cutlass and a rattle in order to sound the alarm or summon assistance. However, the Charlies were often old, infirm and preferred to spend their working hours huddled inside their sentry boxes diligently avoiding their duties.

Liverpool's 'cornermen'. They would hang around on street corners and were infamous for their violence and antisocial behaviour.

By the 1830s, Liverpool's night-watchmen were seen as figures of ridicule by the townspeople. As Shimmin tells us, they were "a terror to nobody and an amusement only to mischievously disposed lads." Known as 'pummelling a Charlie' the adolescents of Liverpool would regularly overturn the night-watchman's sentry box or nail the doors shut (with the watchman still inside). Other miscreants would ply the watchman with alcohol, tie him to a lamppost and run off with his rattle and cutlass. Law enforcement was so ineffectual that eventually the army would be called in to restore order.

Victorian Liverpool therefore must have been a chaotic and noisy place. During the day it would have been a deafening mass of townspeople, street children, travellers, sailors, animals (including packs of stray dogs barking and fighting over territory), stall holders, omnibuses, carts, carriages and goods wagons. At night, the clamour and noise would have continued as shouting and singing from hundreds of carousing revellers competed with the braying of unruly adolescents, swearing and brawling sailors, caterwauling prostitutes and bellowing street hawkers. Shimmin describes a typical Saturday in Liverpool in 1857:

> *"It is now past 10 o'clock on a glorious summer night… and Scotland Road is teeming with a moving throng... there are a number of lazy fellows standing grouped at a street corner, obstructing the thoroughfare and insulting all decent passers-by, here is a basket woman and her sympathisers, she is treating a policeman to some of the choicest Billingsgate for ordering her to move on... there is a street singer... and yonder there is a fight!"*

'A Court for King Cholera'. A typical Victorian street scene in many British cities. Punch Magazine 1852.

Liverpool was not the only city which required a new type of policing in order to control the increasing urban population. In 1836 the government took action by issuing the 'Municipal Corporations Act' which required towns and cities to establish a properly functioning police force like that of the London Metropolitan Police Force which had been formed in 1829. It was on the Metropolitan model that the Liverpool City Police was established.

A Liverpool City Police constable in summer uniform c.1860. Armed with truncheon and rattle to summon assistance. © liverpoolcitypolice.co.uk

The new Liverpool force, which consisted of 290 new constables and officers, aimed for much higher professional standards. The training of new recruits and structure of the force was run on military lines. A 'Watch Committee', which consisted of elected town council members, was appointed to monitor and audit the new police force. A Head Constable was appointed and was expected to regularly report to the Watch Committee on the performance of the new force.

The exact date on which Robert Marsden left his post as a bookkeeper and joined the Liverpool City Police is unknown. He may have decided to apply as, at a time when work in the town was mostly of the 'casual' type, the role of a police officer at least ensured steady employment and a regular wage. To join the Liverpool force, Robert Marsden would first have to meet its strict recruitment criteria. Each applicant had to be at aged between 22 and 35 years and be at least 5ft 8ins tall; to be sober, of 'good temper' and able to pass a medical examination. In addition to physical fitness, each recruit had to be literate and was required to write his own letter of application and provide references to the Head Constable.

When Robert Marsden applied in the 1850s, the Head Constable was Major John Grieg. Grieg conducted recruitment interviews for new police officers every Thursday. Successful interviewees were then officially sworn-in and issued with a uniform. The uniform consisted of a dark blue swallow-tailed coat with each constable's identification number on the shoulder. A thick leather belt with a buckle depicting the Liverpool City Police crest was added. Dark blue trousers were worn in the winter and white in the summer. A leather top hat was also issued. This had two purposes. Firstly, to make the policeman look taller (and hopefully more intimidating to criminals) and secondly to act a protection from head injury. The rest of the uniform consisted of two pairs of boots, two pairs of gloves, an oil skin cape, truncheon, whistle, rattle (to summon assistance from other police officers) and a pair of handcuffs. Finally, a 'Book of Instruction' was provided. This contained eight hundred points concerning by-laws and instructions which the recruit was expected to learn diligently.

Major Grieg. © liverpoolcitypolice.co.uk

Major John James Greig was born in Edinburgh in 1807 and joined the British army aged 21. On his retirement in 1852 he was appointed as Head Constable of the Liverpool City Police. By appointing an army officer, the authorities in Liverpool were attempting to run the new police force as close to military lines as possible. Major Grieg was a religious man and was known to be severe in his dealings with those who broke the law. On Sunday afternoons Major Grieg would visit prisoners in the cells waiting to appear at the Police Court on the following Monday morning. He would sometimes take a clergyman with him and try to explain to prisoners the error of their ways. However, in cases of drunk and disorderly behaviour, he would berate prisoners by bellowing at them in the manner of the parade ground. Major Grieg retired in 1881 and is the longest serving Head Constable of Liverpool.

New Recruits

All new recruits would begin as third-class constables. For the first three weeks in post new constables were placed in a probationary class in which they shadowed experienced police officers as they walked their beats. They also visited the Central Police Court on Dale Street in order to learn how to give evidence clearly in court. Probationers also performed 'drill' in which they undertook intense physical exercises in order to build muscle and strength, 'to open out the chest', and to learn how to use a cutlass and baton proficiently. They also learned how to advance and

keep together when called on to suppress a riot. Drill was also intended to train recruits to work as part of a disciplined team and socialise recruits into police 'culture' (Shpayer-Makov, 2011). By professionalising policing and using military-style training methods, Shimmin tells us that Liverpool policemen had become a body of men with a fine physical appearance and could match many crack army regiments for fitness and discipline.

Working conditions for police constables were extremely tough. They were expected to work twelve-hour shifts, seven days a week. Night shifts were from 6pm to 5am in the summer, or 6am in the winter. Leave was limited to two weeks per year. Wages commenced at around eighteen shillings per week, which for the time, was about the same as that of the average non-skilled labourer. For this wage the new recruit was expected to apprehend criminals and prevent crime, direct traffic, report nuisances,

A Liverpool Police Fireman c1860. © www.liverpoolcitypolice.co.uk

visit beer-houses and pubs to ensure they were not harbouring prostitutes or being run in a 'riotous or disorderly manner'. They were also tasked with:

"bring all cases of cruelty to animals – particularly to working horses before the magistrate, to see that no dogs 'run at large in the month when they are likely to go mad', restore wandering children to their parents, suppress vagrancy, see that none perish from pure destitution and procure medical aid in all cases of accident".

'Drill' with cutlasses. Here performed by Bristol Police.

Constables were also given extra duties as town firemen. Promotion through to first class constable, sergeant, inspector or detective would then be possible for recruits depending on behaviour and aptitude.

Robert Marsden worked in the North Division of the Liverpool City Police; an area encompassing Netherfield, St Anne's, Vauxhall, North/South Scotland Road.

By the beginning of the 1860s, the Liverpool City Police force had become a highly respected body of men. So much so that Charles Dickens applied to join as a 'special constable' for 'research purposes'. In 1860 he accompanied the superintendent and officers on night patrol to the Salthouse and Albert Docks, Liver Street, Canning Place and Wapping. Dickens went on to record his experience in the short story *Poor Mercantile Jack*, published in 1861. He writes that the Liverpool force was:

> "...composed, without favour, of the best men that can be picked, it is directed by an
> unusual intelligence. In Mr Superintendent I saw a tall well-looking, well-set-up man of
> a soldierly bearing, with a cavalry air, a good chest and a resolute but not by any means
> ungentle face. He carried in his hand a plain black walking stick of hard wood; and
> whenever and wherever, at any after-time of night he struck it on the pavement with a
> ringing sound, it instantly produced a whistle out of the darkness and a policeman".

Unexpectedly, many people in Liverpool did not welcome the formation of a new police force, or at best, they saw it as an irrelevance. Criminal behaviour and neighbourhood disputes were seen by many living in poor or slum areas as matters which could be dealt with by their own 'informal' policing. That is, the townspeople would deal out their own form of punishment to anyone committing criminal behaviour within their community. The sight of a uniformed public servant, interfering in the natural justice of their neighbourhood, was seen as evidence of a prying government and a meddling middle-class.

Argyll Street Bridewell, Liverpool.

PROLIFIC JOURNALIST, NOVELIST AND, FOR...

CHARLES DICKENS

BORN PORTSEA 1812 · DIED GAD'S HILL, KENT 1870

SO WROTE DICKENS, WHOSE FIRST VISIT WAS IN 1838. FROM 1842 UNTIL
1869, HE WAS A FREQUENT VISITOR, GIVING READINGS FROM HIS
NOVELS, USUALLY TO LARGE AUDIENCES AT ST GEORGE'S
HALL, ALSO AT THE FORMER MASQUE THEATRE, DUKE
STREET. IN 1860 HE WAS SWORN-IN AS A CONSTABLE
FOR 'RESEARCH PURPOSES'

PLAQUE UNVEILED 17 JANUARY 2004

...ONE DAY IN 1860, LIVERPOOL POLICE CONSTABLE

Plaque commemorating Charles Dickens serving as a special constable with the Liverpool City Police from the Argyll Street Bridewell.

Police detectives (who wore plain clothes) were viewed with even greater suspicion - they were the invisible and unidentifiable government surveillance men - eavesdropping and spying on the working man enjoying his traditional pastimes of drinking, fighting and gambling. Also, in the eyes of the port's large Irish Catholic population, the mostly Protestant police force were treated with further suspicion and resentment. For them, the police represented the oppression and the cruelty of the aristocratic (and mainly Protestant) landowners back in Ireland. In 1857, Hugh Shimmin graphically described the treatment of the average Liverpool police constable by the townspeople when he wrote:

> *"Poor Bobby gets fearfully knocked and kicked about sometimes, and nobody minds. It is all part of his business; what else does he receive his twenty shillings a week for? You may see a policeman in the midst of a crowd struggling with a 'rough'. He is knocked down; he scrambles up again; goes down again; is kicked savagely in the head, in the face, on the shins, on the abdomen; has to fight for his very life… and all the time the crowd looks on cheering, laughing, delighted, as if it were a fight between two dogs…"*

In addition to the Central Police Office and Police Court on Dale Street, the main locations in which Liverpool City Police officers were based were the 'Bridewells' placed around the city. A Bridewell is a police station with prison cells. In the North Division in 1860 these were located at Athol Street, Exchange Passage North, Rose Hill, Esk Street and Vauxhall Road. In 1870 Shimmin wrote a series of articles titled 'The Bridewell Sketches' for Liverpool's satirical newspaper *The Porcupine*. In these he describes his observations during a typical Saturday nightshift for police at Rose Hill Bridewell.

Rose Hill Bridewell where Hugh Shimmin observed a Saturday night shift in 1870. Source: liverpoolcitypolice.co.uk

Bridewell Sketches II and III

"It is ten o'clock on a Saturday night. The first specimen of a Chisenhalian [a resident of Chisenhale Street] we see arrive is walking in at a great speed, in a slanting posture and with an immense shuffling of feet and with the nape of his neck resting against a policeman's knuckles." [The Bridewell keeper takes the prisoner through the door to the corridor containing the prison cells and]: "as the door opens and the whitewashed corridor is seen, a Babel of whistling, singing and shouting comes wafting out. The officer bangs the door and deadens the sound... all the time we stay here it runs like an undercurrent beneath all the talking that is done in the office... The [court]yard door opens and a blue sleeve encircling a big loaf [prisoner] bespattered with blood and mud, intrudes itself. Another spasmodic push at the door and a policeman comes in sideways, pulling after him a drunken and almost senseless woman."

Bridewell Sketches IV

"No sooner does the one door bang... than the other opens on a silent handcuffed group in the [court] yard. They are marched in and the officers proceed to take off the irons. They are now seen to be all young men of the most coarse and brutal type and are not at all enhanced in appearance by their winking to one another as the "darbies" are being taken from their wrists. The officer who states the charge looks rather ferocious when seen alongside the stripped, bleeding ruffians, inasmuch as he bears in his hand a bar of iron nearly as tall as himself, which with a wet crimson blotch at the end of it looks like some sort of a spear he has been doing battle with. For such a purpose, indeed, it has been used by one of the prisoners upon the head of a man who has just been brought in and upon a woman who has already been carried off to a surgeon.

The prosecutor [prisoner], a strong, sinewy fellow, is deluged with blood from cuts to the head. He winces as he sticks his cap firmly on his blood-soaked hair while the prisoners are booked and stands aside as though fearful of them. Whoever the fault lies with, it is clear that he has had a merciless pounding with the bar. The simple tale is that they, all living in one house close-to, have had a little misunderstanding together at home, which induced them to attempt setting matters to rights by throwing one another down the stairs and distributing arguments with an iron bar. Woman-like the female got the worst of the lot, but she had still to congratulate herself on being accidentally left alive."

The Main Bridewell at Cheapside, Liverpool. This closed in the 1990s and is now a luxury hotel and student accommodation.

In view of the dangerous working conditions experienced by police officers, it is not surprising that many recruits resigned from the force within their first year. The long hours on duty, low wages, abuse and assaults from the public plus the temptation to drink in the many public and beer houses along their beat proved too much for many. In other cases, new recruits were dismissed for being drunk or asleep on duty or for simply deserting their beats. Major Grieg claimed that not one in ten recruits remained in the Liverpool City Police after two years; and not one in a thousand remained after ten. To be considered for the position of detective officer, Robert Marsden would first have had to experience the challenging task of working as a 'Bobby' (described above) for a number of years before reaching the position of first-class constable. As only first-class constables could apply to become detectives, it is fair to say that Robert Marsden must have been a man of significant authority, intelligence, physical strength and courage to reach this stage of policing.

Becoming A Police Detective
The London Metropolitan Police created a Detective Department in 1842. From its beginnings, its role was to capture criminals and obtain evidence which would be robust enough to stand up in court. Initially, detectives were known as 'thief takers', but their use as investigators of all types of crime quickly became clear. For central government, plain clothes detectives were important in allowing the state to monitor any destabilising forces or internal subversion which might be brewing in the population. In the middle of the nineteenth century this would have been focused

on the growing trade union movement and on the Irish catholic nationalists, known as the 'Fenians'.

Rochdale detectives, 1875.

Such was the success of London's detective force in meeting these demands, Liverpool City Police Detective Department was established in 1844. By the 1860s this consisted of sixteen officers - one of whom was Robert Marsden. The new detectives were chosen by Major Grieg for 'their sharpness of wit, absolute reliability, thoroughness and steely ability to deal with some of the worst elements of Liverpool society' (Archibald, 2015). Wade (2007) adds that a detective "had to constantly add to his geographical and trade knowledge. He also had to be familiar with a complex street slang and code of behaviour."

> *"Whether engaged in the detection or the containment of crime, a great many detectives spent the bulk of their work time in the open, in areas of squalid deprivation and sordidness, and often in the company of drunks, informers and petty thieves. Seeking evidence or information, detectives frequently entered the 'lion's den' - the "hot" quarters of their divisions."* (Shpayer-Makov, 2011)

Detective Office, Prescot Street Bridewell.

Liverpool's new detectives were expected to trail and apprehend suspects into the most dark, dangerous and squalid of the town's courts and alleyways. These were places which most ordinary people and even beat police constables carefully avoided. Furthermore, once a detective had apprehended a suspect, he then had to walk (or drag) his captive through the streets to the nearest Bridewell. He would often be chased, berated and attacked by the captive's family, associates and even passing members of the public – many of whom would do their best to liberate the prisoner. Detectives often wore plain clothes rather than a uniform and were not averse to using disguises in order track or infiltrate criminal activities.

Metropolitan Police detectives posing in some of their various disguises.

Robert Marsden and his colleagues were given a monthly stipend for 'wearing their own clothes' but whether Liverpool detectives employed disguises is not known. However, they would have found this strategy useful, particularly when trying to apprehend habitual and well-known offenders. As well as their own skills in surveillance and tracking criminals, each detective relied heavily on informants to bring him information.

As a major seaport Liverpool was one of the most common routes by which criminals would attempt to escape the country. It would be important for detectives to be in plain clothes in order to blend with the crowds, while they watched the docks for felons about to board ship. The importance of this is illustrated by the following, taken from *The Graphic* (1872), which describes how the police kept a constant presence at Liverpool's passenger landing stages.

'A Study from Life on Prince's Landing Stage, Liverpool' (1870) Detective Charlie Carlisle can be seen standing with the uniformed policeman on the right of the picture.

"The Prince's Landing stage is seen to the most advantage on the departure or arrival of the great steamers, the variety of the nationalities, for the moment huddled together, the concentration of strong emotions of hope and fear in some, the recklessness and indifference in others, together with the eccentricities of costume, form a tableau which once seen will always be remembered. Passengers are conveyed to the steamers by tugboats from the Prince's Stage; the stolid German emigrant with his frau and children smokes his long pipe as calmly as though crossing the Atlantic to a new home was an everyday incident of his life. Americans with their sharp features, peaked beards, glossy boots and coats, and the everlasting drawl, everywhere predominate, and above all the Babel-like hubbub and apparent confusion, the great steamer's heart throbs impatiently, as though longing to speed away. The calmest and coolest person on board is a tall, well-built man in a shooting suit of grey, whom you would set down as a country gentleman from the midland counties, who appears to take a good humoured rather than a lazy interest in all that transpires. In reality, however, our friend is one of the most experienced Liverpool detectives, known in select circles as "Charlie Carlisle" and depend upon it, if there be a bank forger or a fraudulent debtor on board or any publican or other sinner who has eloped with his neighbour's wife and cashbox, Carlisle will not leave the ship without that particular culprit in his grasp."

(Source: www.old-merseytimes.co.uk/policedeaths.html)

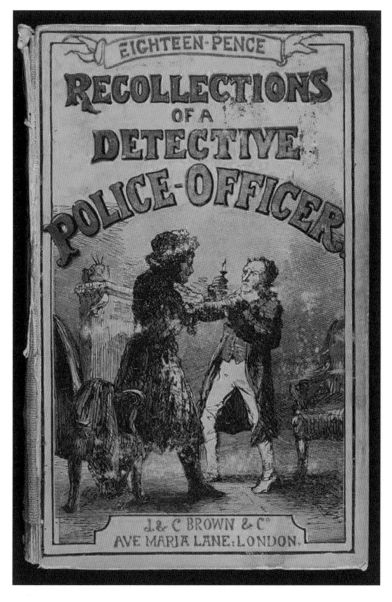

Such was their success in detecting crime and capturing criminals, by the 1860s police detectives were increasingly depicted in the press and popular literature (see above) as individuals with immense powers of observation and unique intuition. Detectives such as Nicholas Pearce of the Metropolitan Police and Jerome Caminada of Manchester Police achieved almost celebrity status. However, the day to day duties and more mundane tasks carried out by most police detectives, such as the surveillance and trailing of suspects, was less often publicised. Fortunately, Liverpool Record Office still possesses an account of a Liverpool detective's duties. Written by the Superintendent of the Detective Department, Laurence Kehoe, to the Liverpool Watch Committee in 1869 it describes a routine Robert Marsden would have been very familiar with. Sadly, the documents and records described by the account, ie., the Borough Robbery Book, Officer's Time Book, Duty Book, Central Police Report Book and Memorandum Book have all since been destroyed either by subsequent police administrations or during the blitz of World War II. However, the following still gives us a glimpse of a typical day in the life of a detective officer in Victorian Liverpool.

Monday 22nd February 1869.
Report of Superintendent Kehoe to the Liverpool City Watch Committee.

"Before proceeding to point out the leading features in the duties performed by the Detective Police, the Superintendent would offer a few remarks as to the mode in which information of robberies is dealt with in the Office. To make the duty in the Detective Office as intelligible as possible, the Superintendent proposes to give the details of a day's work. Every morning the Superintendent first examines the Borough Robbery Book and in a column set apart for the purpose, makes a short memorandum of the steps he directs to be taken in each case. Should the robbery be of a nature to require the services of a detective officer, he selects one, who, from his special experience is most suitable for the particular case.

Communications from the Police not within the Borough, are next attended to and dealt with in a similar manner to the Borough felonies. The duty of the detective officer commences at 9 o'clock a.m. when he signs himself on duty in the book kept for that purpose. Should he have any special duty, he receives from the clerk a copy of the information as to the robbery and the memorandum made by the Superintendent relative thereto. He then enters in the "Officers Time Book" a short account of the case upon which he is about to be engaged and makes a note in reference to it in the "Robbery Book". He proceeds at once to make the necessary inquiries, calling in the first instance, on the person who furnished the report for the purpose of ascertaining whether all the particulars are contained in such report and whether any additional information can be given. It then becomes his duty to trace out the thieves and recover the stolen property. In doing this very much depends upon his experience and ability, and the perseverance and energy with which he follows up the slightest clue.

As it would be impossible to follow the officer from place to place, to see whether his instructions have been honestly carried out, the fullest confidence must necessarily be placed in him as to the employment of his time (and the Superintendent has much pleasure in here stating that seldom has this confidence been misplaced). The officer however is made to feel that it is not merely his duty, but his best interest to succeed, and to leave no stone unturned that may properly bring about that result. Under ordinary circumstances he is expected to call at the Office during the day, and report and to receive any further information which may have been left for him since he first set out. Circumstances however may occur during the course of his enquiry which may prevent this.

At from 7 to 8 o'clock pm he returns to the Office entering in the "Memorandum Book" how he has been engaged and the result; he remains in the Office until 8pm when his duty ordinarily ceases. Should the case however which has been assigned to him be important, and require further and constant attention, he will continue to engage himself upon it, even during the whole of the night. An epitome of the duty performed by each officer during the day is entered in the "Central Police Report Book" which is submitted to the Head Constable for his information every morning. In addition to the entries here mentioned, the reports made by the officers are carefully examined by the Clerk and a minute of the result entered in the Borough or County Robbery Book in the column set apart for the purpose. This, as a matter of reference, is found necessary and is most useful in showing the steps taken and the result in each case.

It not infrequently occurs that young constables receive into their custody persons charged with serious offences, in which the evidence is difficult to be obtained or of a complicated nature. In such cases a detective constable is detailed to assist him. This is of advantage not only to the service, but to the inexperienced constable, who from the mode adopted by the detective officer in conducting the enquiry, has the opportunity of being initiated in a most important part of his duty. Whenever practicable, the younger detective constables are associated with their seniors, for the purpose of receiving instructions in the best and safest methods of performing duty; in some cases however this arrangement would operate prejudicially, especially in extensive cotton robberies. Clerks and others absconding with large sums of money, and other important cases, when it has been found to be of advantage to employ those officers who have been accustomed to work together, and who have a speciality for such cases.

On occasions such as races, Easter and Whitsun holidays, cheap excursions etc., when large numbers of strangers are attracted to the borough, many of who are found in the streets at night more or less intoxicated, it is then found necessary to employ detective officers up to a late hour in patrolling the streets, to watch well known or suspected characters there being at such periods a considerable influx of thieves from London, Manchester and other principal towns.

In commercial communities like ours, applications are frequently made for the assistance of the police by merchants, brokers, wholesale traders and extensive employers of labour for the purpose of investigating cases when large sums of money and valuable property have been embezzled or stolen. These are amongst the most delicate and difficult cases the detective police have to deal with, for as a rule, the persons are unable to point to any particular individual as being concerned in the offence. When there are reasonable grounds to suspect that a felony has been committed, or is in process of being committed, a suitable officer is selected who generally traces the guilty person.

In most of these cases the services of the [detective] constable are required either before or after the ordinary hours of duty. In conclusion, the Superintendent would beg to remark that he is fully impressed with the advantage of detective officers possessing a moderate amount of education, but at the same time it must be observed that there are other qualifications required which take precedence even of that, namely – absolute reliability, which can only be determined by knowledge of each man's character during several years and also police experience which is equally necessary and this of itself has become almost a profession.

Close observation is made by Superintendent to the Police Court, as to the manner in which the ordinary constables behave before the Court; the most intelligent of such are selected for special duties in the Central Police Office, during the absence of the detective constables at Assizes and Sessions. These men are employed upon the less important cases of the department and gradually acquire, by such training, a moderate knowledge of detective duty. When vacancies occur the selections are made among them, the promotions however are still held over for some time, that a further period of probation may be passed through." (Liverpool Records Office, Liverpool Libraries)

The dangerous nature of detective work is pictured in 'Captured trying to shoot two detectives'. Illustrated Police News, 25th January 1868.

CHAPTER 2

1859-1860

On 31st October 1859 Robert Marsden makes his first appearance in a published newspaper in his role as a detective officer. Newspapers such as the *Liverpool Mercury* and the *Liverpool Daily Post* published daily reports regarding the more interesting or sensational cases which appeared before magistrates at the Police Court on Dale Street. It appears that Robert began his detective career investigating cases of embezzlement and 'larceny' (ie.,theft of personal property), fraud and pilfering by the local population. This is in keeping with duties described by the Superintendent Kehoe in the previous chapter, in which newly appointed detectives are given less serious cases to begin with.

THE NORTHERN DAILY TIMES
31st October 1859

SERIOUS CHARGE OF EMBEZZLEMENT.—A respectably attired person about forty years of age, named John Hart, who was described as residing at 44, Crown-street, was charged with embezzling various sums of money, the property of Messrs. Fletcher and Co., tobacco manufacturers, Fleet-street.—Detective Officer Marsden stated that when he told the prisoner the charge, he said he was guilty, and that he had been carrying it on for seven years.—Mr. Fletcher said the prisoner had been in their employ as head clerk for the last ten years. It was his duty to go to St. Helen's two days every week, to collect accounts and make a return of what he received. He had been there on the 13th, but he had given no account of £100 he received from Mr. Blinkhorn, of St. Helen's. The sums traced to him at present amount to from £800 to £1,000 They had the greatest confidence in him—as much as though he had been a partner. The prisoner was remanded for a few days.

LIVERPOOL DAILY POST
29th February 1860

PILFERING- Thomas Redmond, a youth about twelve years of age, an assistant in the shop of Mr. Brown, pawnbroker, Great George's-place, was brought up by detective-officer Marsden, on a charge of pilfering from his master. A variety of articles were found which were identified, and Mr. Brown said he had also lost 10s in money on Saturday. Among other purchases of the youth was an illustrated copy of "Jack Sheppard" [a fictional highwayman]. He was remanded for seven days for inquiry.

The article above names a Mr Raffles as the magistrate before whom Thomas Redmond's case was heard. Raffles was a prominent member of Liverpool's law enforcement community and he was the officiating magistrate on many cases in which Robert Marsden was involved during the 1860s.

TS Raffles, Liverpool's Stipendiary Magistrate.

Source: liverpoolcitypolice.co.uk

Born in London in 1818, Thomas Raffles was appointed stipendiary (paid) magistrate for Liverpool in 1860. He was described as 'just, humane, popular, affable and pains-taking.' During his thirty-year career he would preside mainly at the Liverpool Central Police Court. On Monday mornings he would typically hear the cases of 100-250 prisoners (mostly drunk and disorderly from the previous Saturday night). On other days of the week the average would be 60 cases. Mr Raffles died in 1891 at his home in Abercromby Square, Liverpool age 72.

Liverpool Central Police Office and Police Court, Dale Street (opened in 1865). It later became the Liverpool Magistrates Court. It closed in 2015.

Dale Street c1860 (WG Herdman)

By the 1860s British police courts were infamous for their scenes of riotous and chaotic behaviour. *The Porcupine* featured a series of articles describing scenes from Liverpool's Police Court. Detective Marsden would have been a familiar figure amongst the police officers giving evidence during hearings.

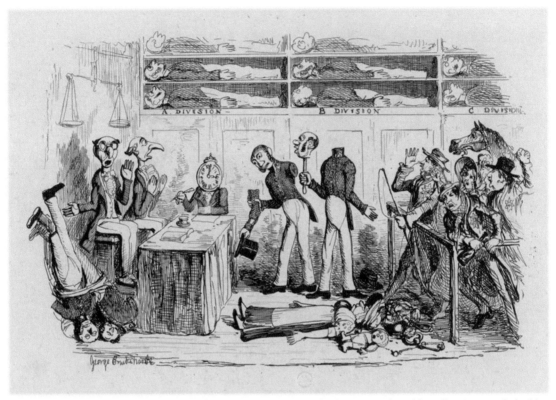

'Automaton Police Court and Real Offenders' (G. Cruikshank). Rowdy observers in the public gallery irreverently heckle as police give evidence to a magistrate.

A police constable giving evidence in a Magistrates Court.

THE PORCUPINE
Scenes from the Liverpool Police Court.

If ever there was a small pandemonium on earth, the lobby of our Police Court merits that distinction. Children screaming, women making them worse by beating them to keep quiet! - the women themselves abusing each other in tones and fancy language that would make a fortune for John Camden Hotton or any other compiler of a slang dictionary. The atmosphere as well as the inhabitants of this locus is redolent of positive immorality, and in a sanitary point of view it is amazing that a plague does not emanate from it. The air is thick and is composed of a villainous compound of smells - of decomposed tobacco, bits of mouldy bread and many other things. It is astonishing that fever of the worst type does not break out and carry off everyone about the place, for the moment one of the court doors opens, the rush of polluted and dangerous air is fearful and nearly stifling... The jabber, the blasphemy, the foul epithets hurled about, are bad enough, but added to this is the seething crowd and the steaming, filthy atmosphere which they create. There is nothing like it to be seen or felt throughout England. The moment a prisoner is put to the bar, that prisoner be he man, woman or child (of the latter there are, unhappily, too many) the people behind the reporters box stand up and crowd over to the back, causing much inconvenience... the odour reminds one of the Virginian weed and alcoholic liquids rather than of a field of Persian roses or the spice valley of Ceylon. At the same time as the persons alluded to rush to get a sight of the prisoner, the people in other parts of the court stand on tiptoe, and some jump up on the back seats and one can see them straining their necks almost to dis-jointure; trying to catch sight of some poor little hungry boy, the apex of whose head is several inches below the top bar of the dock. This unhappy orphan seems to attract much more attention there than he did outside, for the charge against him is for running away with an apple or an orange, or, under the imperative pressure of hunger, he may have scampered off with a penny cake.

Illustrated Police News. 26th May 1895

A Detective Partnership Begins

Throughout his career, Robert Marsden often worked in partnership with other detectives. In 1860 this was an officer named Redman. Newspaper reports from 19 May and 7th July 1860 feature Marsden and Redman investigating two novel cases which involved the surveillance and arrest of two individuals suspected of fraud. The cases highlight the popularity of that peculiar Victorian obsession with the supernatural – and in this instance with the practice of clairvoyance. Fortune telling was at this time illegal as in law it was classed as fraud. However, the business of telling fortunes could be a lucrative one and it attracted a large number of opportunists who were willing to run the gauntlet of local law enforcement in order to make money.

In the first of the following cases, a clairvoyant named Richard Parkinson – who went by the name of 'the Wizard' – comes before magistrates. He ran a fortune telling business from his home in Roscommon Street, Everton. However, by 1860 he had become the subject of a number of complaints made to the Liverpool City Police by disgruntled townspeople. Liverpool's Head Constable, Major Grieg assigned the case to Detectives Marsden and Redman, and it is here, for the first time, that we hear Detective Marsden's voice being directly quoted as he gives evidence in court.

Incidentally, this report is also valuable as its describes, at first hand, the ribald and noisy scenes from the Police Court's public gallery (as described previously). Both the literal and ambiguous language used by Detectives Marsden and Kehoe is not lost on the crowd of spectators and newspaper reporters present. Their reactions and laughter reveal that, like today, there was a popular taste for innuendo and double-entendre.

THE NORTHERN DAILY TIMES
Friday 11th May 1860

THE FORTUNES AND MISFORTUNES OF RICHARD PARKINSON. - Richard Parkinson, a small man, apparently about sixty years of age, whose face resembled the head of an overgrown eel, was brought up by officers Marsden and Redman, on a charge of having swindled Caroline Harrison, a married woman, living at Edge-hill, and Anne Smith, a milliner, residing in Great Howard-street, out of a shilling each, under pretence of telling their fortunes. The case caused a good deal of attention. The prisoner resides at No, 1 Bala-terrace, Roscommon-street, and it was stated that he lived in excellent style.

Marsden said: "in consequence of certain letters and communications made to Major Greig, I along with Redman, went to the prisoner's house, at half past six and after a short time we saw one of these ladies go into the house, and in about half-an-hour she came out, when we told her to stop for a short time. In a few minutes after, Miss Smith went in. I followed her, and ran upstairs, where I found the prisoner sitting at the window and Miss Smith sitting opposite him. He had some apparatus belonging to a galvanic battery in his hand, and she had a hold of it too." (A burst of laughter from the spectators in the courtroom followed.)

-Marsden: "I heard him tell her to hold it tight." Here he [Marsden] produced a long three-sided piece of heavy glass, a glass egg-shaped ball, and a glass globe, all solid, the exhibition of which caused renewed laughter. -Marsden: "When I ran in, he (the prisoner) pulled this sword of glass out of her hand and put it between his legs to hide it." (Great laughter.) "I caught hold of him, and asked, why did you not prophecy that we were coming to catch you'?" (Renewed laughter.) "We will tell your fortune for you." "Oh, said he [Parkinson], I don't care a pin about you, for I have been with an attorney, and I don't tell fortunes now, as I only sell them papers telling them about herbs

46

and that sort of thing." -Marsden: "I then arrested him, and Miss Smith seemed in a terrible state about her fortune being told. When we came down, we saw some ladies dressed in silks and satins come up to the door, who were going to have their fortunes told; but we had taken up the prophet, and we promised to tell them his fortune to-day." (Roars of laughter.) Here he again exhibited the galvanic glasses, amid another shout of laughter.

Officer Redman produced a lot of books which he found in the house. Some were in manuscript, and some printed. The former were incantations of a most outrageous and blasphemous description. There were also some bills about herbs and the like, and these the prisoner sold to his patients for a shilling each in order to avoid being prosecuted for obtaining money by false pretences, for telling fortunes. The officer also said he knew that the prisoner got three months' imprisonment, in Mr. Rushton's time, for telling fortunes. He got a letter, of which the following is a copy: "Augusta, aged 19 the 30th August last. Please look in your glass and tell me all you can see likely to happen to me, either good or bad. A shilling's worth of stamps enclosed. Address the two letters enclosed to Mrs. Vedal, who has kindly enclosed these for us."

-Mr Kehoe [Detective Superintendent] then called Caroline Harrison, a handsome young married woman, and asked her, "what is your husband?" The witness laughed heartily, and then replied, "I don't know." (Great laughter.)-Mr. Kehoe: "What! Don't you know what your husband is?" Mrs Harrison: "Well, he is no particular trade." Mr. Kehoe: "Is he a gentleman, then'?" "Oh, no, I think he may be a tailor." (Roars of laughter.) -Mr. Kehoe: "What did you go to the prisoner's house for? Mrs Harrison: "Why, I went partly out of curiosity, and paid him a shilling, and I don't think it was thrown away." Mr. Kehoe: "Well, then, you went there to enquire something about your husband's gallantry?" "Something of that sort, I believe." (Great laughter.) -Mr. Kehoe: "Well, go on." Mrs Harrison: "He got

one of those glasses and put it in my hand then he looked through it, and said he could very plainly see that my husband was a mate of a ship and that he was coming to me in about a week or so, but if I did not mind him he would go off with another woman - like winking." (Roars of laughter) "He said that when my husband's money was nearly gone he would cut with the other young lady. He told me to watch the docks for three days and my husband would come home then and to stick to him." (Renewed laughter.) "I gave him a shilling for looking through the glass, but I could not see anything, and he said it was only particular persons who could see through that glass." - Mr. Kehoe: "Is your husband a seafaring man?" "Not at all, sir." Mr Kehoe: "Then all the prisoner told you was untrue? "Yes, every word that he told me was a lie from beginning to end." -Mr Kehoe: "What sort of a house is it?" Officer Marsden: "It is a very elegantly furnished house".

-Anne Smith, a bashful looking young lady, a milliner in Great Homer-street, said: "I went to the prisoner's house out of amusement, I don't know for what else. He gave me the glass and then gave me a paper, and I laid a sixpence on a glass plate." -Mr Kehoe: "Did you ask him to tell you anything?" "No, for I thought he knew what I came about better than I did." (Laughter.) Miss Smith: "When I looked through the glass, he said it was rising most gloriously. (Shouts of laughter.) Mr Kehoe: "And did it rise gloriously?" "I don't know, for at that instant the police came in and gripped him, glasses and all". (Renewed roars of laughter).

This was the evidence for the prosecution. The prisoner, in reply to the charge, said it was not half the truth the witnesses told against him. The ladies came to him, as hundreds of others did: they used to tease him most wonderfully to tell their fortunes, and what could he do but comply? He could not help it, if they came to him. He sold them charms for herbs, and that was all. The two female witnesses here said the prisoner gave them some papers and said they were charms for husbands and sweethearts. It was proved that in 1853 the prisoner got three months' imprisonment for telling fortunes. Mr. Raffles said the prisoner was an idle, silly, and, he feared, a blasphemous old man, and he wondered how people at this time of day could be found so foolish as to go to him for fortune telling purposes. Officer Marsden said he saw six ladies, all in silks and satins, coming up to his door. Mr. Raffles sent the prisoner to gaol for three months, with hard labour.

THE NORTHERN DAILY TIMES
30th June 1860

FORTUNE-TELLING EXTRAORDINARY. A WELSH PROPHETESS IN JEOPARDY. Yesterday, at the morning sittings at the Police-court, before Mr. Raffles, a Welsh woman named Sarah Roberts, alias Owens, alias Williams, was brought up by detective-officers Marsden and Redman, charged for having obtained money under false pretences, by assuming to tell fortunes. Mr. Bluck [solicitor] was for the prisoner. The case created some interest.

Officer Marsden said: "In consequence of a letter received by Mr. Ride, one of the superintendents of police, I, along with officer Redman, went on Monday evening to watch the house of the prisoner, at 45, Finch-street; we watched that day and evening, and also on Tuesday. We went again yesterday (Thursday) between two and three o'clock and saw two ladies go into the house—one of the ladies is here. We waited until they came out, and then we asked them if they were getting their fortunes told? and they said they were, and that the prisoner had given them a piece of printed paper, which contained receipts for cleaning re-irons, furniture, glass, etc.— (laughter) —and charged them one shilling for it. We then arrested the prisoner."

[Marsden] Cross-examined by Mr. Bluck: "We were at the house before yesterday, and saw ladies go in and come out. We had no conversation with this lady here before she went into the house; I don't know if the two ladies paid money to the prisoner, but this lady says she paid her 1s." -Mr. Bluck: "Oh, but that was for the receipt for the fire-irons and you know that is very valuable." (Laughter.)

-Witness [Marsden]: "I found a cup with tea dross in it, which she had been tossing up, to tell the fortunes of the ladies. (Laughter.) —I then took the prisoner into custody, and told her the charge was for obtaining money under false pretences, then she showed me her legs, which are much swelled (laughter)—and begged hard for mercy, and said if we did not lock her up, she would leave the town at once. We found £5 in money, and a receipt from the bank for £160, where she has it lodged."

-Mr. Bluck: "Did you not find a letter from Mr. Snowball relative to some business?" -Witness [Marsden]: "Yes, I got a letter there that he had written to someone, threatening to bring an action against someone whom the prisoner alleged was annoying her by hanging out clothes on a line. (Laughter.)

-Mr. Kehoe: "Did you find out anything about cup tossing?" -[Marsden] "Oh yes, the lady here will tell you all about that." Detective-officer Redman corroborated the statement of Marsden, and added, "I found a number of cards and letters. Amongst the letters, there was one from a Miss Mary H. Higginbotham, Dillman-street, Ashton-under-Lyne, enquiring about her fortune, and stating that the writer would recommend her to a great many good customers in that locality. Another letter from the same young lady, who, from the style of her composition and the character of her writing, must be a person of intelligence and education; and this was an apology to "My dear Miss Roberts," for not writing before, in reply to one from the fortune-teller, "but really she could not until Pa and Ma left town, and then she seized on the first opportunity to return her love, and to ask for any further luck in her fortune since the last letter." Another letter was from Sunnyside, from Anne Salisbury, informing her "dear Miss Roberts, that she had certain dreams about a gentleman, who used to visit a certain house, and who used to stare at her in the most provoking manner. She wished to know if there was any chance of her being married to that staring gentleman, or to any other gentleman this year." "Another epistle was from some man signed himself "W. Ridgway, Chester." This gentleman, it would appear, expected a visit from "dear Miss Roberts," and had a phaeton and pair prepared to meet her, but she disappointed him, " most awfully." It would also seem that his peculiar anxiety to meet the Welsh prophetess was about his wife, but he " was glad to inform Miss Roberts that his better half had presented him with a fine boy, and both were well". The officer also said he found a copy of the *Daily Times* with a report of the case of Parkinson [see previous article], who was sent to gaol, a short time since, for three months, for "fortune telling," or rather for having swindled some young women out of money under false pretences. In that paper were found a quantity of cards and other things pertaining to the black art."

-Margaret Nicholson, a handsome, smart, and modest-looking young lady, stated: "I live in Parron-street, Edgehill, and am married. I went to the prisoner's house yesterday, between two and three o'clock; I knew where to go, for I had heard a great deal about her before, as a fortune teller. When I went in, I asked for Miss Roberts, and she said, "I am Miss Roberts." I asked her what her charge was." -Mr. Kehoe: "For what"? Witness: "Oh, she knew that, I suppose. I asked her what she charged for telling fortunes. She said a shilling." Mr. Kehoe: "I suppose you considered that to be a very moderate charge?" —The witness put on a bland smile, that made her look more handsome than she really was, although, as stated, she is very pretty.

She went on to say —"I had heard a great deal of talk about her as a fortune-telling prophetess before, and I went to see if she knew anything." Mr. Kehoe: And did she tell you a great, deal?" Witness: "No, she could not tell me anything." Mr. Kehoe: "I thought so. But tell the magistrate what she did tell you." Witness: (laughing and blushing red as an opening moss-rose): "Why, she told me I would soon be married to a gentleman who was under the Crown." (Laughter) Mr. Kehoe: "Is that true?" Witness: "No, for I am married already." Mr. Kehoe: "But then she must not have known that you are already in the happy fetters of matrimony—had you your ring on?" "No, I took it off before I went into the house. The prisoner told me that if I had my fortune told on the cards, it would be sixpence, but if she tried the teacup, it would be a shilling. (Great laughter.) Mr. Kehoe: "Did she toss the tea-cup?" "Yes, she tossed the cup, first putting some tea into it out of a measure that had already tea made in it. Mr. Kehoe: "What she did she say when she tossed the cup?" "She said there was a great crowd coming, (laughter,) and told me a great many things."

-Mr Kehoe: "What did you ask her?" "I asked her about a certain party, and she said he was coming back soon with a great deal of money, and that I would be married to him all right." (Laughter.) Mr. Kehoe: "Did she say what colour he was, blue, white, red or green?" (Roars of laughter) "She said he was of exceedingly, fair complexion." Mr. Kehoe: Do you know anyone of that description?" "Not one in the world. I paid her a shilling for the cutting of the cards and the tossing of the cup. She turned the latter round and round, and said she saw a large bird coming with great good news in its mouth." Mr. Kehoe: "Anything else?" "Yes; she said she plainly saw a ring and two hearts joined very closely." (Roars of laughter.) "Did she say whose hearts they were?" "Oh, not at all." Mr. Kehoe: Did she say, anything else?" "Yes; she said she saw a great peacocks feather, and that I was on the spree next week. (Great laughter) Mr. Kehoe:

"And are you going on the spree next week?" "It is more than I know at present, if I am". Mr. Kehoe: Did she say where you were going on the spree, and how long you were to remain on it?" "She said I was going to New Brighton, but how long she did not say. She spoke about Parkinson, who was a convicted here of fortune-telling and said, if any detectives asked me anything, I was to say she was only writing a letter for me."

Cross-examined by Mr. Bluck, Mrs Nicholson: "I am six months married. I did not go to inquire about my husband." Mr. Bluck: "What did you go enquire about?" "Nothing in particular; but I heard so much about her I thought I would go and see and hear what she had to say. The lady who was with me is married, but she is not here. She did not give the prisoner any money."

Mr. Bluck then made an appeal to his Worship on behalf of the prisoner, urging her ill state of health, and said she promised to leave the town at once if discharged. —Mr. Raffles sent her to gaol for one month. —Mr. Bluck applied for an order to have her property taken care of as she had a great deal of valuable goods in her house. The Police said the property be taken care of. Mr Raffles said he would order the money for her maintenance to be stopped out of the money found in her house. — This prophetess is about 60 years of age, not of forbidding appearance. She was rather handsomely dressed.

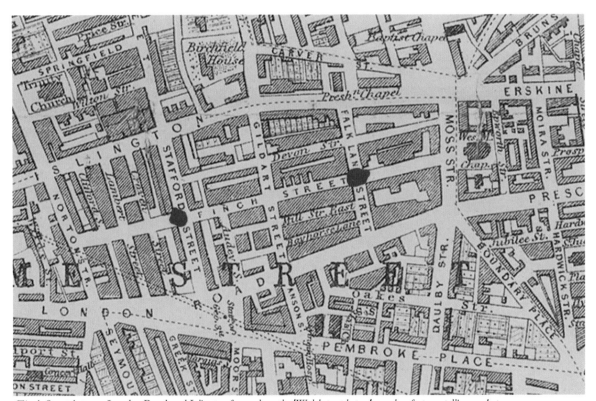

Finch Street between London Road and Islington from where the 'Welsh prophetess' ran her fortune-telling racket.

The next group of cases in which Detective Marsden features are those concerning the capture and prosecution of two housebreakers (burglars) from North Wales. They had been operating in Liverpool for some time.

THE NORTHERN DAILY TIMES
28th November 1860

CAPTURE OF TWO WELSH BURGLARS. Owen Jones alias Pritchard, a desperate looking ruffian and James Green, were brought up by Mr. Jones, (a clerk in the Detective Office), and Detective Officer Marsden, on the following charge. Mr. Bluck (solicitor) appeared for the prisoners. Mr Jones said: "at half-past three yesterday, I received information that two men were in a house in Hatton Garden, looking for skeleton keys, and that they were suspicious persons. I went there along with officer Marsden and saw the prisoners in the back-part of Mr. Challoner's shop. I asked them what they wanted with the screws? [slang name for skeleton keys], and they could not tell. I asked them where they came from? They refused to tell; and then Green took off a scarf he had on and tore it up. We then arrested them as suspicious persons." Inspector Horn said, "when the prisoners were brought to the station they were searched, and about £22 or £23 got on them. We got, amongst other things, a piece of paper on Pritchard, on which were the names of Mr. Springman, Grove-park, Lodge-lane, and. Miss Ross, Cherry Cottage, Lodge-lane, and we suspected the prisoners had "set" these houses to rob them. Your worship will hear evidence on that point.

On looking over the books and *Police Gazette*, we find, that Pritchard is "wanted" in Wales, for having committed several burglaries and robberies there and in England. There is a full description of him here, and it appears that he has broken out of Ruthin gaol. Mr. Bluck: "That has nothing to do with him at present."

Officer Marsden said: "I arrested Pritchard, and found a glazier's diamond and a knife on him, and £6 3s. in money. I also got this paper with two addresses in Lodge-lane on it. I went to the house of Mr. Springman, Lodge Lane, and asked for a Miss Pritchard, and found there was such a person there as cook. I asked her if she knew a man named Jones? and she got into a great flutter and was confused. I told her not to deny it, and asked her if anyone had been to see her lately? and she then said two men had been to see her, and that one of them (the prisoner Pritchard) was her brother, but she did not wish him to come there anymore." Mr. Bluck objected to this evidence, as it had nothing to do with the prisoner. Mr. Horn repeated that the prisoner was wanted on two or three charges, and he was described as being in company with an Irishman. Mr. Bluck again objected and asked his worship to discharge him. Mr. Raffles said there was not the least chance of his doing that.

Mr. Challoner, of Hatton-garden, said: "the prisoners called at my shop, and asked for some screws. What sort of screws? said. I, and they pointed at some skeleton keys. I suspected all was not right, and said I was making some, and if they came back at half past three, I would have some ready. I then sent for the officers, and when the prisoners came back, I showed them into the back, and kept them till the officers came to take them into custody. Mr. Raffles: "You acted very properly." Marsden said he got a quantity of new silk handkerchiefs on the prisoners. Mr. Raffles: "Let them be remanded for seven days".

The criminal trial of Jones (alias Pritchard) and Green is next to be reported. It appears they had been operating in Liverpool under various different alias' during 1860. In his final newspaper appearance for 1860, Detective Marsden travels from Liverpool to Wrexham Magistrates' Court in order to give evidence against the two prisoners (whose real names were Owen Pritchard and Daniel Ryan). Owen Pritchard in particular had been convicted for robbery a number of times and had previously escaped from Ruthin Gaol. Again, in this report we hear Robert Marsden directly quoted as he gives evidence in court.

Illustrated Police News, 28 November 1868.

THE NORTHERN DAILY TIMES
8th December 1860

WREXHAM COUNTY MAGISTRATES COURT.

TWO NOTORIOUS CHARACTERS. Owen Pritchard and Daniel Ryan were in custody charged with burglary. Mr. Edwards, of Ruthin, appeared for the prosecution. After giving an outline of the charge, he called Evan Roberts, who said —"I live at Chwileiriog, near Llandegis.   On Sunday, the 4th of November, I had about £35 in gold in the house. It was in brown holland bag. There was also little silver in the bag not a pound's worth of silver. There were also nine or ten crooked sixpences in drawer, and six or seven bad half-crowns in another drawer. There was a great coat, too, hanging in the lobby, and an Alpacca umbrella. Also a part of ham and some tea. I went over the house before going to bed. I locked the parlour myself. The cupboard in the kitchen was also locked. We were not disturbed at all in the night. There were two servant men in the house. In consequence of information that I received in the morning, I went downstairs between six and seven o'clock. I found the parlour door wide open. There was no harm done to the lock. The bureau had been opened, and the papers strewn about the floor. The bag of money was gone. The umbrella was also gone. The kitchen cupboard was unlocked. A perforated zinc pane had been torn out of the cellar window, by means of which the window had been opened and an entrance effected. There was no lock on the cellar door. I examined the premises outside the house and saw the tracks of men. There had been more than one man there – I think two or three. Prosecutor then identified a coat found upon one of the prisoners as the coat he had lost from the lobby on the night of the robbery.

Robert Marsden was next called. He said "I am a detective officer in Liverpool. I apprehended the prisoners on Monday, the 26th ult., in Hatton Garden, about half past three in the afternoon. They were getting keys at Mr Chaloner's – a second-hand ironmonger's shop. They were both together. Prichard was the first that I saw. I put my hand in his pockets and in the left-hand pocket I found a glazier's diamond and some small pieces of glass. I took the prisoners to the Central [police] Office and searched him. I found a purse, and in it this slip of papers with the following address written on it- "Miss Pritchard, Mr. Springman, Grove Park, Lodge-

lane, Liverpool." On the other side of the paper was written "Miss Ross, Cherry Cottage, Arrow Park, Woodchurch, Cheshire. There was also £6 5s 6d in the purse. On Ryan I found two purses. In one of these was £16 in gold, and in the other £1 12s 6d. On Ryan I found the coat sworn to by the witness Roberts. He had also a silver watch and guard and some other articles which I now produce."

Both prisoners cross-examined this witness in a very impertinent manner, but they did nothing to shake his evidence.

Thomas Williams, a little boy eleven years of age, deposed to having seen the prisoners at his father's house at Bwlch Gwyn, one Sunday, about six weeks ago, in the afternoon. His father keeps a public-house, and they had tea there. The prosecutor said this public-house was five or six miles from his house, by the road, but there was a much nearer way across the open country. Detective officer Marsden said he found two watches upon the prisoners— one worth £2 and the other £5. Both prisoners manifested great effrontery during the examination, which ended by their being committed to take their trial the next assizes. After they were committed, Mr Rymer said he had a charge of stealing brass from Lwynennion, to prefer against the prisoners, and he should like the evidence taken down. The magistrates declined to enter into any other case the prisoners could be indicted at the assizes for any other offence.

CHAPTER 3

1861

By 1861 Robert Marsden was consolidating his role as a detective police officer. In the following cases, it can be seen that as well as detecting crimes already committed, he was also involved in crime prevention. During this year he continues to work with Detective Redman and (the soon to be famous) Detective Carlisle (see *Liverpool and its Steamfleets*, Chapter 1).

THE LIVERPOOL DAILY POST
14th February 1861

THEFT OF JEWELLERY BY A DOMESTIC SERVANT. Frances Taylor, a young woman who formerly lived as a servant in the house of Mr. Louis Nathan, jeweller, of Mount Pleasant, and who had been remanded on the charge of having stolen quantity of watch guards and other jewellery from the house of her master, was again brought before the court. The prisoner, who had lived in the service of Mr. Nathan for more than four years without any suspicion having attached to her, a few weeks ago got married an officer of the Wigan police force. She left her situation, and went temporarily to lodge with a Mrs. Wright, in No. 2 Court, Edmund Street. In consequence of some information given Mr. Nathan, he communicated with the police. Detective officer Marsden was instructed to search the prisoner's lodgings. He found there a number of boxes packed up, and ready for removal to Wigan. On searching these he found a quantity of gold watch keys, guards, and other articles of jewellery, and two pawn tickets having reference to other similar articles pledged; and on a subsequent occasion found eight other pawn tickets.

—Mrs. Wright, the person with whom the prisoner had gone temporarily to reside, deposed to having pledged for the prisoner a number of articles of jewellery at the shops of Mr. Perry, Messrs. Critchley and Deverill, Mr. Syred, &c. The property was produced and identified by Mr. Nathan, and by Mr. Levi, a gentleman who lodges with him.

—The total amount of the property was stated to about £45, and the prisoner was committed for trial. At her subsequent trial, Frances Taylor was found guilty and sentenced to 4 years penal servitude.

Victorian Criminal Punishment: Prison and Penal Servitude.

The trial of Frances Taylor (above) and her subsequent sentence to four years 'penal servitude', raises the subject of punishment of condemned prisoners during the mid-Victorian era. With the introduction of the 'Penal Servitude Act' in 1853, prisoner transportation to the British colonies of Australia and Canada became less common and was replaced with a punishment known as 'imprisonment with hard labour' or penal servitude. For the Victorians, penal servitude served a number of purposes. Firstly, imprisonment removed criminals from the streets and reduced their opportunities to commit further crime. Secondly, it was meant to punish and break the will of even the most hardened offender. Finally, it was meant to act as a future deterrent, the argument being that the experience of prison should be one which was so awful for prisoners, they would never want to return to such a place again.

At the beginning of their sentence, prisoners were often placed in solitary confinement (known at the time as 'separation and silence' or the 'silent system') for the first weeks or months. The official reasons given for this was to allow them time to reflect on their crimes and also to separate them from the negative influence of other prisoners. Prisoners were allowed to leave their cells once per day for exercise and for chapel, but no contact or conversation between prisoners was allowed. To heighten this, they were required to wear face masks or hoods (pictured). The aim of this type of 'sensory deprivation' was to reduce prisoners to a state of isolation and docility.

Once the separation and silence phase was complete, prisoners were put to work. The work was designed to be physically and mentally exhausting, the aim being to avoid idleness and emphasise the idea that everyone must work for their keep (as opposed to living off the taxpayer or the proceeds of crime whilst serving their sentence). The tasks prisoners were given were extremely strenuous, monotonous and often completely pointless.

The Tread Wheel. This consisted of a large hollow cylinder of wood on an iron frame (rather like a waterwheel) with steps attached. Several prisoners at a time would continuously climb these steps using their weight to make the wheel revolve. In some prisons the wheel was used to grind corn, but in most it was not used as anything other than as a completely aimless task. Prisoners would usually tread the wheel for ten minutes, with five minutes rest in between, for up to ten hours a day. A set number of steps had to be completed before prisoners were given their meals.

The Crank. This device was simply a large encased drum filled with sand or gravel. On the outside of the drum was a handle which the prisoner turned; this was attached to a cog which pushed a paddle through the sand. This required some effort to make one turn and it rapidly became an exhausting task. A counting device attached to the handle recorded the number of turns the prisoner made.

Prison warders were able to tighten the crank, making it harder to turn, which gave them their nickname of "screws". Most prisoners had to complete 10,000 turns a day. Prisoners who did not achieve this would not be allowed their next meal or even to go to bed.

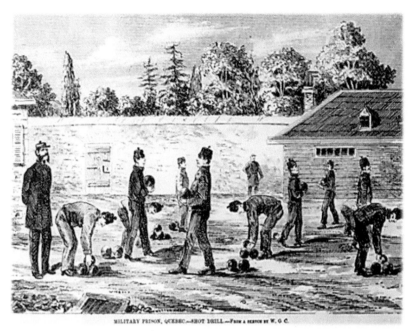

MILITARY PRISON, QUEBEC.—SHOT DRILL.—FROM A SKETCH BY W. G. C.

Shot drill. Originally a form of punishment performed by the military, shot drill involved the prisoner carrying a series of cannon balls or rocks, one at a time, from one pile across the exercise yard to another. The prisoner would then walk back to the original pile and repeat the task. When finished the prisoner would then return the cannon balls or rocks from the second pile back across the prison yard. This exhausting task would be performed repeatedly for a number of hours per day.

Picking Oakum. This form of punishment was most often performed by imprisoned women and children or those living in workhouses. It involved picking or separating tarred rope into its individual fibres so it could be used again. Separated oakum was mixed with tar and was used by the navy to line ships' hulls making them watertight. This task was extremely tough and prisoners' hands and nails would often crack and bleed.

CHARGE OF HARBOURING THIEVES AND PERMITTING DRUNKENESS AGAINST A PUBLICAN. Henry Woodward a publican, 14 Thurlow-street appeared in answer to four summonses—three charging him with harbouring thieves of notoriously bad character, and one for permitting drunkenness in his house. Mr. Deighton (solicitor) instructed by Mr. Roby appeared for the defendant. Detective-officer Marsden stated that ten minutes to eleven o'clock on the evening of the ult. He visited the defendant's house, where he found John Berry, James Taylor alias "Nipper,' a person called "Jack" runner for George Glover, (a receiver of stolen property), and three other men, the whole of whom are thieves. Witness [Marsden] told the defendant that the men were thieves, and that if he allowed them to remain he would summon him for harbouring thieves. At twelve minutes past eleven o'clock on the same evening the witness [Marsden] called at the house again, and found therein Berry, Taylor, "Jack," and three other thieves.

— Detective officer Redmond corroborated the statement of Marsden.

—For the defence, Mr. Deighton said the words of the license were "Knowingly permit or suffer persons of notoriously bad character to assemble and meet together therein," and it was for a breach of that clause that the defendant was summoned. There was, he contended, no evidence to show that the defendant knew that the men found in his house ware thieves, or that there was anything about the detectives to lead him believe they were policemen.

The next question was: "Did the defendant know that the men found in his house were notoriously bad?" He held that a person to be a notoriously bad character must be a person who was well known to be such to the public, and not simply known as such to the police. The third point was: "Did the defendant allow these men to meet and assemble together?" On each of these points Mr. Deighton held that his client had not brought himself within the meaning of the Act.—The magistrates said they had no doubt but that the defendant knew the men were thieves, and inflicted on him a penalty of 40s. and costs.

—The second, summons against the defendant was for harbouring notoriously bad characters on the evening of the 15th ult. Detective officer Marsden said he found in the house, at a quarter to eleven o'clock, a number of thieves, whom were Berry, Taylor, Rafferty, Jones, French, and Elizabeth Thumb. He called again in a quarter of an hour and found the same persons in the house. Mr. Deighton, on being asked what had to say in reply to the charge, remarked that it would be useless to ask the bench to ignore their previous decision. The magistrates inflicted a penalty of 60s and costs.

-The third information was laid by Inspector Carlisle, who said that at quarter past eleven o'clock on the evening the 16th ult., he found in the defendant's house eleven men and four women all of whom were professional or travelling thieves. The evidence was corroborated by Detective-officer Scott and other officers. The bench thus inflicted a penalty of £5 and costs. The summons for permitting drunkenness was dismissed. Mr. Brighton then applied the bench for a case to take to the Court of Queen's Bench. After some consultation, however with Mr. Wybergh, the magistrates refused the application.

'Burglars Carousing'. Punch Magazine, 1850

THE LIVERPOOL MERCURY
13th March 1861

DISGRACEFUL CASE OF ROBBERY.—Gavin Hamilton, a well-dressed young man, who fainted soon after he was placed in the dock, and trembled fearfully throughout the hearing of the case was brought up on charges of having stolen a watch and jewellery, together of the value of shout £45, money amounting £15 and a quantity of wearing apparel, belonging to Captain Magna, of the American ship 'David Hudley'. The prisoner shipped as a passenger aboard the vessel for the voyage from New York to Liverpool. The passenger was appointed steward and became acquainted with the stewardess to whom he was married on the ship arriving at this port in December last. Captain Magna was taken seriously ill during the passage and the prisoner and his wife attended on him during illness. When the ship got into port the captain went to reside at the house of Mrs. Wilson, Dublin-street, and the prisoner and his wife subsequently took apartments in the same house, in order, they said, that they might be near to the captain, and give him proper attention during his sickness. Hamilton absconded from his lodgings on 2nd February taking with him gold watch, a diamond breast pin, diamond ring, two gold sleeve links and quantity of wearing apparel valued together at £45. He also carried off £48 in money, £38 10s. which was the amount of the bill of Mr. Evan Thomas, surgeon, for

Detectives apprehend a felon about to escape by train. Detail from 'The Railway Station' by William Powell Firth c1871.

attendance upon Capt. Magna and medicine. This sum having been entrusted to him for the purpose of discharging the account. After absconding from the house in question, Hamilton was traced by the police from one boarding house to another, but they did not succeed in apprehending him until yesterday morning, when, in consequence of information given to them, detectives Marsden and Graham went to Lime street railway station, where they found the prisoner and his wife just about to depart by the seven o'clock London train. They had a considerable quantity of luggage in their possession, and on the officers examining it, the detectives found amongst it the wearing apparel that had been stolen from Captain Magna. The Captain's gold watch and the whole of the stolen jewellery were found upon the person of Hamilton, together with £37 14s 71 in money. The property having been identified as belonging to Captain Magna, the prisoner, who said nothing in defence, was committed for trial.

THE LIVERPOOL MERCURY
7th May 1861

BURGLARIOUS ENTRY OF A DWELLING HOUSE. —An ill-looking fellow named Thomas Jones was brought up on the charge having burglariously entered the house of Thomas Hill, 67, Seacombe-street, Everton, and stolen a pair of galoshes and a knife. For some weeks past a number of robberies have been committed at dwelling houses in Great Homer-street and the neighbouring thoroughfares. These depredations have generally been committed on a Saturday night, the thieves evidently taking advantage of the inmates being at the market or shops making their purchases. On Saturday night last Detectives Marsden and Redman were scouring the locality indicated, on the look-out for evil-doers.

About half-past three o'clock on Sunday morning, on passing along Seacombe-street from Netherfield Road North to Great Homer-street, and on passing the house in question, Marsden noticed the pane of glass in front of the catch of the cellar window was broken and directed Redman's attention it. They then called up the inmates of the house and informed them that it was not safe with the window in that condition, at the same time they inquired if anyone had broken into the premises. The inmates not only ridiculed the idea of such a thing but behaved uncivilly towards the detectives for calling them out of their beds "for nothing." They said no one could get into parlour from the cellar, and as to what there was in the latter, they did not care.

A few minutes after the officers left the premises, however, Mr. Hill inquired of the servant girl if the cellar window was in the state described when she went to bed. On her telling him it was not, he made examination of the lower part of the premises. In the scullery he found a light burning and the prisoner crouching beneath the slop stone. He was speedily hauled out by Mr. Hill and one of his lodgers, when he pretended to be intoxicated. He was very soon handed over the care of the police, when he said he was drunk and was not aware that he had got into the house. He was now remanded for seven days in order that inquiries might made about him.

Seacombe/Seacome Street, Everton scene of Thomas Jones' ill-fated burglary. This photograph was taken shortly before the street was demolished in the1960s.

BIGAMY. — A respectable dressed middle-aged man, named James Macpherson, an engineer on board a steamship, was charged at the Police Court Liverpool, on Saturday with bigamy. It was proved that, in 1851, the prisoner was married to Euphemia Patterson, at St John's Church, Waterloo, Surrey, and that he had since been living away from his wife for some years. Ann Rowlandson, a smart-looking young woman, who said she lived in Smith Street Kirkdale, stated that she was married to the prisoner on the 28th of March last, at the church at Walton-on-the-Hill. She did not know at that time that he was a married man — he had represented himself as a bachelor; but in about six weeks after their marriage, he told her that he had been married, but he believed his wife was dead, though he could not say positively. In consequence of that statement, they made inquiries which resulted in the discovery of the first wife, who was living in the north of England. Detective Marsden, who apprehended the prisoner on board his vessel at Greenock, informed him that his wife was not dead, to which he replied, " I thought so." The man, in his defence, alleged that, in the Court of Session, Edinburgh, an action for divorce had been commenced against his first wife, but the inquiries of the police showed that proceedings had been instituted for the purpose stated, but had not been carried to a final issue. The prisoner, who also urged that he was not aware that his first wife was still alive, was committed for trial at the assizes on the charge of bigamy.

THE LIVERPOOL MERCURY
12th November 1861

GARROTTE ROBBERY IN THE STREETS.
A young fellow, William Bonus, apparently a dock labourer, was charged with having with other men garrotted and robbed Carl Fritz of £3, a bunch of keys, and other articles, Thursday night last. The prosecutor is a ship's carpenter and resides in Earle-street. According to his version of the affair, on Thursday evening he went into a public house Oldhall-street, where he met with the prisoner and two other men and got into conversation with them. Sundry subjects of interest to himself were discuss and he paid for glasses for the men. They adjourned to a second public house on Oldhall-street, where again Fritz paid for the drink. They left the house in company at twelve o'clock. It appears that they had been discussing the merits and ability of certain eminent pugilists, and that Mr. Fritz must have expressed his admiration of the "noble art of self-defence," for as they got into the street Bonus and his friends inquired if he would like see a little sparring. He said he should. They proposed to take him to a sparring room, and he consented go. They walked along the street together until they came a dark by-lane, where the prisoner seized him the throat, threw him down, and held him so that he could not speak, whilst the others rifled his pockets, having done which, they all ran off. Information on the robbery was given to the police, and on Friday the prisoner was apprehended by Detective Marsden in Lowthwaite's Flagyard, Old Hall-street.

When charged with the assault and robbery, he said, "I was with the men, and had some drink with them, but I know nothing of the robbery." The prosecutor positively identified him as the man who seized him by the throat as stated, and witnesses from the public house, referred proved that he was in company with Fritz on the night in question. The other men have not yet been apprehended, and Bonus was remanded for seven days.

Old Hall Street where William Bonus was apprehended by Detective Marsden for the garotte robbery of Carl Fritz.

THE LIVERPOOL MERCURY
4th February 1861

GAROTTE ROBBERY.-A girl of the town, named Mary McCann, alias Mary Ann Connor 17 years of age was brought up on the charge of being concerned in garrotting and robbing William Carr of £2 13s.

The prosecutor is in the employ of Messrs.- Tyson and Richmond, soap manufacturers, Blackstock-street. On Saturday night he had been at the Adelphi Theatre, and on his way to his home in Earle-street passed through Ben Jonson-street. In the latter thoroughfare he was accosted by the prisoner, and whilst talking to her he was seized by the neck in the garotte fashion by one of two men, whom he had previously noticed standing at a short distance from himself and the woman. He was thrown down, McCann then put her hand into his pocket, and took out his purse and money. Carr caught hold of her dress, and held her a short time, but becoming exhausted, and the pressure upon his neck being tightened, he loosed his hold, and the men made off. On recovering himself, Carr proceeded to Rosehill police-station and gave information of the robbery, with a description of the woman, who was known to the' police. Detectives Marsden and Fitzsimmons apprehended McCann soon afterwards in a Court in Comus-street, styled by the fraternity of thieves "Upper Canada".

A garotte robbery taking place.

Carr now positively identified the prisoner as the woman who robbed him, and she was committed for trial. The men have not yet been apprehended.

Court off Comus Street where Detective Marsden apprehended Mary McCann for her part in the garotte robbery of William Carr. This picture was taken in the 1930s © Liverpool Records Office, Liverpool Libraries.

The Garotte Crime Wave of the 1860s

A caricature of the many anti-garrotting devices in vogue during the Victorian 'garrotting panic'. Punch Magazine 1856.

In 1862 James Pilkington, Member of Parliament for Blackburn, was garrotted and robbed within sight of the Houses of Parliament. This incident set off a panic in the capital and was seen by the Victorian media as evidence of a sinister new twist in methods used by criminals to rob citizens in the street. Garotte robbery was not new in Liverpool and was a well-tried method for criminals to divest newly paid sailors of cash and valuables as they walked in streets near to the docks. In fact, Scotland Road with its pubs, beer-houses, markets and brothels had become a 'hot spot' for robbing sailors in this way. The *Cornhill Magazine* had described garrotting as a 'science' in that it required two to four assailants working in unison. The first task was to identify a victim. They had to be seen as some way vulnerable or easily deceived. In some cases, a female accomplice who acted as a lure by appearing either distressed or soliciting was used (as in the case of William Carr, above).

Whilst the target was drunk or distracted, a gang member would approach him from behind and using either his hands or a crooked arm around the throat would apply pressure until victim blacked out. The rest of the gang would then rifle the casualty's pockets. The scene would end with the victim left lying in the street and the assailants running off into the myriad of dark alleyways and courts of Liverpool's slum district.

Garrotte robbery was perceived as different to other forms of theft in that it did not involve weapons and rarely rendered victims permanently injured. However, it was seen as particularly horrifying, and stoked by the assault on James Pilkington and subsequent media coverage, the country became gripped by 'garrotting panic'. However, with the passing of the 'Garrotters Act' in 1863, which made the crime punishable by flogging, incidents of these offences rapidly declined.

CHAPTER 4

1862

1862 seems to have been a quiet year in terms of newspaper appearances for Detective Marsden. His wife Elizabeth gave birth to their seventh child, Georgina, in April of that year. Georgina was baptised on 3rd September (at Christ Church in Everton). Sadly, she died of bronchitis four days later and was buried at St Mary's Church, Walton-on-the-Hill (pictured) on 10th September. Georgina's death highlights how precarious the first years of life could be at this time. There were forty burials at St Mary's Church during the week in September 1862 when Georgina Marsden was laid to rest. Of these burials, twenty-nine (three quarters) were for children under the age of 5. The cause of death in the majority of cases was diarrhoea followed by scarlatina (scarlet fever), croup, convulsions, 'decline' (or failure to thrive), measles, pneumonia, diphtheria and 'atrophy'.

Whilst the Marsden family mourned the loss of Georgina, crime continued to challenge the authorities in Liverpool. One particular problem, synonymous with most major seaports at the time, was the culture of fighting with the use of knives, particularly amongst ships' crews whilst on shore leave. In January 1862 Major Grieg reported the problem to the Liverpool Watch Committee and made a proposal as to how to combat this.

Report by the Head Constable to the Liverpool Watch Committee
January 26th 1862

The Head Constable has the honor to lay before the Watch Committee a communication from the Clerk of the Magistrates enclosing a resolution of the Justices relative to handbills being printed, in various languages, to be distributed to ships entering the docks, boarding house keepers and others. Cautioning seamen from carrying on their persons sheath knives, to use of which in broils [fights] has in many cases led to fatal results. (Liverpool Records Office, Liverpool Libraries)

Sailors were infamous for their drinking and violent behaviour in Liverpool during the nineteenth century.

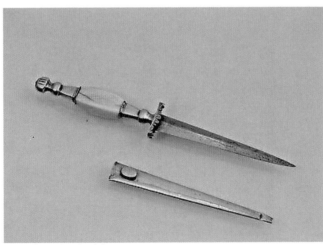

A traditional sailors' dagger.

"The dagger was the traditional weapon of the docklands, capable of transforming petty arguments into murder enquiries. Liverpool sailors routinely carried sheath-knives or clasp-knives while some foreign seamen favoured stilettoes. Most smokers also carried penknives to cut up tobacco. However, foreigners, particularly Mediterranean and South American sailors, were said to have a different cultural attitude towards knife fights." (Macilwee, 2011)

1862 is significant for Robert Marsden as it sees the beginning of a detective partnership with fellow officer William Fitzsimmons. This proved to be a very successful collaboration which lasted for a number of years. The first case in which the partners appear together in a newspaper report is that of the Lace Street burglary. At this time Fitzsimmons is still a police constable (probably first class) and will be become a detective officer by November of that year.

BURGLARY. -Three young fellows, named Michael Costello, Thomas Lawson, and James Sweeney, were charged with breaking into the' shop, of Mrs. Griffiths, grocer and provision dealer, No. 55, Leece-street, and stealing about £25 in money. The prosecutrix closed her shop at a quarter-past eleven o'clock on Friday night, and the next morning it was found that the place had been broken open and the money named, which was in a till or drawer, stolen. An entrance had been effected by the cellar door, the bolt by which the latter was secured being close to a window. A pane of this window had been broken, and the bolt of the door then pushed back. In consequence of information obtained by the police, the prisoners were suspected of having committed the burglary. Detective Marsden and police-officer Fitzsimmons went in search of them, and apprehended Costello in a house in No. 16 Court, Ben Jonson-street When charged with the robbery Costello at, once said "I'm one of them" admitting that he had committed the burglary in company with the other prisoners. When the latter was taken into custody one began to "split" on the other, Sweeney asserting that Lawson and Costello had broken the window and entered the prosecutor's premises, and that they had given him £3 as part of the proceeds of the robbery. Lawson also made a statement with the 'view of showing that he was not so deeply implicated in the transaction as the others, though he did not deny his participation in the robbery.' One of the prisoners had purchased a quantity of new clothing with a portion of the proceeds of the depredation. None of the money had been recovered, and the prisoners were remanded for seven days.

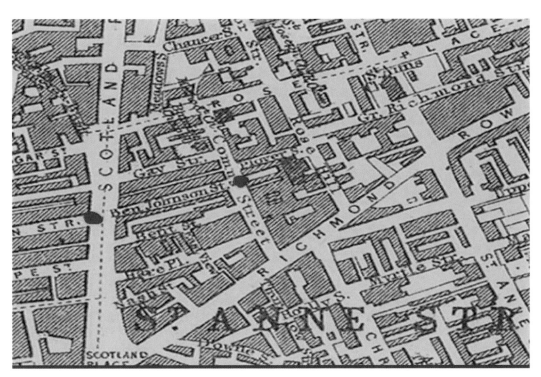

Ben Jonson street off Scotland Road where Detective Marsden apprehended burglar Michael Costello.

Ben Jonson Street: The Most Notorious in Liverpool.

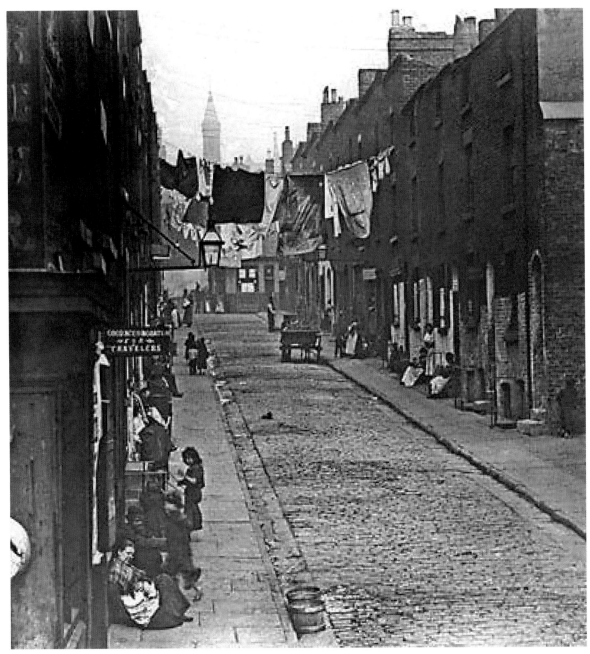

Ben Jonson Street (home of burglar Michael Costello in the previous case) was one of the most notorious in Liverpool for poverty, overcrowding, disease and crime. In this picture, mothers and children can be seen sitting on doorsteps and pavements. This was a common sight in poor communities as it allowed women to watch their children and exchange gossip with neighbours. Each of the houses pictured will have been divided between a number of families (probably with one family in each room, including the cellar). Ben Jonson street alone was home to over 1,000 people. Even in the summer, houses here were cold, damp, dark and infested with vermin; many families preferred sitting on their doorsteps and in the street to sitting inside. During the summer families would sit out until 2 and 3am.

After marvelling at the magnificence of Liverpool's newly-built Albert Dock during the 1850s, Hippolyte Taine (a French historian) described his horror on visiting the port's slum districts close by afterwards:

> *"Every stairway swarms with children, five or six to a step, the eldest nursing the baby; their faces are pale, their hair whitish and tousled, the rags they wear are full of holes, they have neither shoes nor stockings and they are all vilely dirty… What rooms! A threadbare strip of oilcloth on the floor, the old idiot grandmother crouches in a corner; the wife is engaged in trying to mend some wretched rags of clothes; the children tumble over each other. The smell is that of an old-clothes shop full of rotting rags…" (Hippolyte Taine)*

Lionel Street. Poor families spent most of their time sitting on doorsteps as an alternative to the cold, dank interiors of their homes

William Booth, founder of the Salvation Army, proposed that one of the reasons why so many men crowded into the town's public houses each night was not only because these places provided warmth, light and the anaesthetising effects of alcohol; they also provided an attractive alternative to the cold, dark and squalid conditions of their homes. Liverpool journalist, Hugh Shimmin also recognised this. Writing in 1868, he suggested:

> *"look at the bright lights, the costly decorations, the beaming visages behind the bar, the steaming mixtures which are handed to the jabbering crowd, and think of the dark court, the dull misery-stricken house; the wife lean and vixenish, the children pallid and ragged." (Shimmin, 1868)*

A Sunday Afternoon in a Gin Palace (1879) Artist Unknown.

In the next case in which Detective Marsden is featured, the link between crime and the type of desperate poverty experienced by people living in Ben Jonson street is brought into sharp focus.

LIVERPOOL MERCURY
17th July 1862

ROBBERIES BY WORKMEN AT A RICE MILL,- James Kenzie and Patrick Foy were placed in the dock charged with having stolen four bags of rice, of the value of about £4, from the rice mill of Messrs. Wakefield and Ash, Soho-street. Kenzie was defended by Mr. Cobb, and Mr. Ward appeared on behalf of Foy. On the 27th of June last, Joseph Horace, a carter in the employ of the Skelmersdale Coal Company, was delivering a load of coal at the prosecutor's mills, and when he had discharged he was asked by Kenzie, who was the foreman there, to take four bags of rice to the house of Foy, one of the workmen, residing at No. 4, Paul-street, and he did so.

In consequence of something which transpired subsequently, the man Horace, thinking that there was something wrong in the transaction, gave information, which ultimately was communicated to the police. Detective Marsden and another officer searched Foy's house, and found four bags of rice concealed beneath the stairs. The bags were identified by a workman in the employ of the prosecutors as their property.

-Having been given concordance with the forgoing facts, Mr. Cobb intimated that after such overwhelming testimony it was impossible to resist the charge. Kenzie had hitherto borne a good character, and he hoped the magistrate would deal summarily with the case. -Mr. Ward urged in mitigation of the offence that his client had acted under the direction of his foreman. Both prisoners pleaded guilty and a gentleman (understood to be the manager of the mill) said they each had a wife and family, and the prosecution did not wish the men to be severely punished. The magistrate remarked that it would not do to let an offence of this description pass without inflicting severe punishment. He had no doubt if the prisoners were sent to the Sessions they would get double the punishment he was able to give them. The case against Kenzie, being the foreman at the mill, was of a more aggravated character, and he must go to prison for six months. Foy was sentenced to three months' imprisonment.

This case, in which four bags of stolen rice flour results in two men being sent to prison for three and six months respectively, highlights the severity of the Victorian penal system. Although the manager of the mill did not wish to press charges against the two prisoners (because they had dependent families), the magistrate chose to prosecute in order to make an example of them and to follow the letter of the law. The consequences of this theft would have been painful for the two prisoners (remembering the methods used in Victorian gaols outlined in Chapter 1) and disastrous for their families. Without their main breadwinner bringing a wage into their home, the wives and children of these men would have been reduced to applying for poor relief, the workhouse or resorting to further crime in order to survive.

THE LIVERPOOL MERCURY
29th November 1862

HARBOURING DISREPUTABLE CHARACTERS - Edward Burns, beer-house keeper, Edgar-street, Scotland-road, was summoned for harbouring thieves and prostitutes in his house on the night of the 20th inst. Mr. Walter appeared for the prosecution and Mr. Cobb on behalf of the defendant. Mr. Walter cited the statute under which the information was laid and which stated that no person should knowingly admit into his house or suffer persons of notoriously bad character to remain therein. Detective-officer Marsden stated that on the night in question he visited the defendant's house in company with another officer, and found there several persons, prostitutes and thieves. Four men whom they pointed out to the defendant were all thieves, and the women were all prostitutes. They visited the house again at ten o'clock, but there was only one of the persons still in the house- "Billy McHugh". Detective-officer Fitzsimmons deposed that one of the men in the house was locked up that same night and had been sent to gaol for a month for stealing a shawl from a shop in London-road. - Mr. Cobb said thieves and prostitutes must live, and if they could not assemble in a refreshment house or beer house, then the Act of Parliament was passed for the purpose of starving them. He maintained, however, that it was never intended that the Act should be enforced in the way it was there sought to put it in force. There ought to be some proof of a real *bona fide* meeting or assembly. If it were proved that they had assembled in the house for some improper purpose, then that would alter the case. The bench dismissed the case, saying they were very far from wishing to discourage such attempts to support the law, but they must take care that they did not overstep the proper bounds and assume as evidence things not proved. The case was dismissed because it was not sufficiently proved that the parties had assembled in the house within the meaning of the Act; but the defendant would see the precipice he was upon, and it was the mere want of evidence which had prevented their fining him very severely.

CHAPTER 5

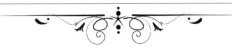

1863

THE LIVERPOOL MERCURY
23rd February 1863

CHARGE OF STEALING AND RECEIVING TEA.- A young man named Thomas Collins, apparently a porter or labourer and Patrick O'Dea, who keeps a provision shop in Titchfield-street and is a collector for St. Patrick's Burial Society, together with Bridget O'Dea, supposed to be his wife, but whose exact position in his house did not seem to be clearly defined, were charged - the former with stealing a half chest of tea, and the two latter with receiving the same knowing it to have been stolen. It appeared that on Thursday, the 19th instant, Thomas Wilson, a carter in the employ of Messrs. John Pepper and Co., agents for the Great Northern Railway Company, was proceeding along Milton-street with a waggon and horses, amongst other goods in the vehicle being a half chest of tea, directed to Messrs. Bailey Brothers Great Homer-street.

In Milton-street a, man directed the attention of Wilson to the prisoner Collins, who was in the act of taking the half chest of tea in question from the wagon. Before he had time to pull up his horses the thief had carried the tea into an entry and placed it in a donkey cart standing there. Wilson bolted after him and having recovered the tea made no effort to capture the thief. Passing on to Marybone, Wilson invited the man who informed him of the attempted robbery to have a glass of ale. As they were coming out of a public house, Wilson saw Collins in the act of again taking the chest of tea from the wagon. He made an alarm, and sundry policemen went in pursuit of the prisoner, but he managed to get clear out that time.

In consequence of some information furnished to the police, on Friday Detectives Marsden and Fitzsimmons proceeded to the house of O'Dea in search of the stolen property. Marsden inquired of O'Dea if he had purchased anything lately. The latter pointed to some tea upon the counter, saying he had purchased it off Mr. Warland, Great George-street. The officers then went upstairs and secreted under the bed they found the female prisoner, the chest which had been taken from the waggon by Collins, and a loaf of sugar, which had also been stolen. On searching a clothes box belonging to O'Dea they found in it a quantity of tea which had been taken from the chest alluded to. When asked to account for his possession of the tea found upstairs, O'Dea, said he knew nothing about it. The woman Bridget was not his wife. He was a collector for St. Patrick's Burial Society, and was often away on business connected with it, when she looked after the shop and bought things. O'Dea had previously spoken of the woman as his wife, and she called him her husband. When they were taken into custody, she said to. him "Oh, Pat', you are guilty of all this." The prisoners were all committed for trial. Michael Foy, a young man was then charged with stealing the loaf of sugar found under the bed from the shop door of Mr. William Smith, grocer, Tithebarn-street, and O'Dea and his wife with feloniously receiving the same. It was proved that Foy had been seen to take the sugar from the prosecutor's shop-door, and the prisoners were all sent for trial.

Tithebarn Street in 1843 (WG Herdman)

Tithebarn Street in the early 20th century. In this picture a herd of sheep can be seen being driven to market.

THE LIVERPOOL DAILY POST
24th April 1863

THE CHARGE OF STEALING POTATOES. STEMMING THE "FLOODS". —George, Julia, and Eliza Flood, an amiable family who have been in the habit for a length of time of swindling persons out of their property by means of sundry dodges under the name of carrying on a "firm" [swindle] were brought up on remand charged with having stolen several loads of potatoes. Mr. Campbell appeared for them. Three cases only were gone into. The prisoners are known to the police as "The Long Firm." They are not particular to the line of business they go into provided a profit can by "worked" out of it.

For some time past they have pursued the potato trade, and their mode proceeding was this:- They fixed upon some unoccupied cellar, which they rented for a short time. They then went into the wholesale markets and having bargained for and agreed to purchase from some farmer a load or loads of potatoes, they ordered them conveyed to some one of the cellars they had rented and there delivered. Having thus got possession of the potatoes, the female branch of the arm commenced to play their part in the little game of swindle, and they generally proceeded with the carter to the weighing-machine, for the purpose ascertaining the weight of the cart, and under pretence of paying for the goods supplied. This was invariably a shuffling operation on the part the Misses Flood, and occupied considerable length time, the ladies usually inviting the carter to take a drink, and in other ways incurring delays. They would then inform him that it would necessary for him to go with them to some supposed bank, which they would name, and this was generally situated at some considerable distance, in some district of the town where streets would tend to "bother" a stranger. During the progress to the "bank," Julia and Eliza would manage to give the bewildered carter the "slip;" and the return of that individual to the cellar where he had left his farm produce, would invariably find it "shut up". The male prisoner, having during the time his amiable sisters were playing their part, removed the potatoes, and sold them anywhere and anyhow he could. The prisoners, in some instances, offered "dollar notes" and "bank bills," which were not, of course, worth the paper they were printed upon.

By the means above sketched out, the prisoners obtained a load of potatoes belonging to Henry Harrison, a farmer residing in Devonshire Place, Everton; another from Thomas Hurst, farmer, Simonswood [near Kirkby]; and another from Edward Frith, farmer, of Hightown. The three loads of potatoes they sold to Mrs. Collins, provision-dealer, 39 and 41, St. James's-Street, for £15 12s. Information having been given to the police from the persons who had been "done" out of their potatoes, Detective police-officer Marsden apprehended the prisoners on Wednesday week at a cellar 31 Denison-Street, after a fight, in which the women fought as women will. The prisoners were committed for trial.

"After a fight in which the women fought as women will".

The 'stemming of the Floods' case highlights a side to Victorian women with which we may not be completely familiar. It emphasises the extent to which women engaged in the type of fierce behaviour which was endemic in inner cities of the nineteenth century. As Detectives Marsden and Fitzsimmons attempted to arrest the Floods in their Denison Street cellar, the final sentences of the article tell us that Eliza and Julia were not prepared to go down without fight. (Detective Fitzsimmons is not mentioned in this particular report but was with Marsden when the Floods were discovered in the cellar).

Archer (2011) tells us that: "women were thought to engage in particularly vicious and 'unfair' methods of fighting. Hair pulling, scratching and biting to name but three were commonly regarded as female… Women appear to have grabbed whatever was close at hand when stepping up to a fight." Whilst on 3rd January 1848, the *Liverpool Weekly Albion* reported that "women engaged in hand to hand fights and the Police Court each Monday morning exhibited a mass of blackened eyes and broken heads, showing how the Sunday had been spent." With these images in mind, the arrest scene in the cellar can only be guessed at.

The ferocity with which some women fought is depicted here in 'Liverpool Savages' © *The British Library*

Dennison Street where Detectives Marsden and Fitzsimmons fought and arrested the Flood family.

HOUSEBREAKING IN EVERTON.-Joseph Lee, Edward Rogan, James Higgins Daniel Murphy, Margaret Hill, Jane Pendleton, and Mary Ann Davis, all young persons, were brought up on the charge of breaking into the house of Mr. Henry Plimmer, No. 11, Lansdowne-place, Mere-lane, Everton, and stealing wearing apparel, books, and other articles, of the value of about £15. It appeared from the statement of Mr. Superintendent Kehoe and the evidence given that Mr. Plimmer is a widower, and about ten days ago left his house, in Lansdowne-place, to reside with a friend in York-terrace, Everton. The house in Lansdowne-place, which was completely furnished, was locked up no person being left in charge. About noon on Monday, Jane McDowell, a servant at the next house, occupied by Mrs. Robinson, saw one of the prisoners, whom she afterwards recognised as James Higgins, in the act of opening or attempting to open a back window of Mr. Plimmer's house, two other young men being in a passage near. The young woman also saw these fellows carry away a box and other articles, Higgins having just previously dropped from the wall at the rear of the premises.

This circumstance seems to have been communicated to her. Mr. Plimmer made an examination of the house, and found that an entrance had been effected by a back window, and that the house had been completely ransacked, the locks being broken off the chiffonniere and drawers, and some of the contents of the latter being carried off. Mr. Plimmer at once made the police acquainted with what had occurred, and the case was placed in the hands of Detectives Marsden and Fitzsimmons, who quickly traced the property and apprehended the thieves. In the evening of the same day they apprehended Lee and Rogan at a singing room at the Globe public house in Willamson-square and found upon them several articles which were subsequently identified by the prosecutor as his property.

The officers then proceeded to two disreputable houses in Atkinson-street and Grenville-street, where they found the remainder of the prisoners, and teapots, books, and other things which had been stolen from Mr. Plimmer's house. Hill had sold one of the stolen teapots to a beer-house keeper for 1s. 9d., and other articles had been pawned.- Mr. Kehoe having asked for a remand, the prisoners were remanded accordingly.

Williamson Square where Detectives Marsden and Fitzsimmons apprehended Lee and Rogan in a singing room at The Globe tavern.

THE CHARGE OF STEALING AND RECEIVING COTTON. -Julia Toman, the wife of a marine store keeper in Pall-mall, and Robert Fernie, who keeps a sack and bag warehouse in Smithfield-street, were brought up on remand the former charged with stealing 210lbs of cotton, belonging to Messrs. Armstrong and Berey, of Hackins-hey, and the latter with having received the cotton, knowing it to have been stolen. William Bowsher, the keeper of the prosecutors' warehouse in George-street, Oldhall-street, locked up the place, in a which a quantity of Sicilian cotton is stored, about five o'clock on Saturday evening, and about ten o'clock on Sunday night was called to the warehouse by a policeman. He found that the door of the bottom room had been broken open, and some 230lbs or 240lbs of cotton carried away. Police-officer No. 418, one of the warehouse patrol, examined the door of the prosecutors premises at seven o'clock on Sunday evening, when it appeared to be secure. At 20 minutes past eight he found that it had been broken open and then informed Bowsher, the keeper of the place.

Information of the robbery having been given at the Central Police Office, Detectives Marsden and Fitzsimmons were directed to make the customary investigation, and they were not long in discovering that on Monday morning the female prisoner took three bags of cotton to the warehouse of the prisoner Fernie, and that they were afterwards hoisted to an upper room of his premises. He was out when the cotton was taken there, but the woman Toman had an interview with him shortly afterwards. Detective Marsden obtained a sample of cotton stored in the prosecutors' warehouse and went with Fitzsimmons to Fernie's premises about eleven o'clock on Monday a morning. The prisoner came down to them from the second floor, and Marsden asked him if he had bought any cotton of that description, showing him the sample. Having examined it, Fernie said a woman had offered him a sample, for which she wanted 2s. per pound but he would not buy it, as it was too dear. He added, "Wait a minute, I want to go upstairs." He went up and returned in a minute or two. Marsden then asked him if he would be so kind as to tell them what sort of a woman it was who offered the sample. He said he believed that she was a woman out of Key-street, but he had not seen her before she looked like an Irishwoman. He again went upstairs, and Marsden stepped to the door, when Fernie, who seemed to be in a very excited state, called out, "Go inside; go inside." He again came downstairs, and Marsden told him it was no use playing with him and his companion; that they were detectives and had come there to inquire about some cotton that had been stolen and that they would have to search his premises. Fernie then said, "Just wait a minute; I want to pay a bill," and again went upstairs.

Whilst he was there Marsden saw pieces of cotton falling through the hatches from one floor to the other. This aroused his suspicions, and he and Fitzsimmons went upstairs. Fernie then told them that he had bought the cotton but had not paid for it. He did not know the woman of whom he bought it, but he thought her name was Toman, and that she lived in Pall-mall. Fitzsimmons, who had gone to an upper room, called out to Marsden to come up. He did so, accompanied by Fernie, and there found a number of women engaged in mixing dirty cotton with clean. Fernie asked for the cotton that came in that morning and told the women to cease the operation they were performing. The clean cotton was put into bags, and Marsden requested Fernie to go with him to Pall-mall and see if he could find the woman in question. They found the female prisoner at her husband's marine store and Marsden told her she was charged with breaking into a warehouse in George-street and stealing cotton. She said some young men came there about half-past seven o'clock that morning and asked her to buy some cotton; that she did so, agreeing to pay them £6, but

£4 for the material. A sample of the cotton found at his place was now produced, and Mr. Joseph Orme, warehouseman to the prosecutors, was of opinion that it was of the same description as that stored upon their premises. Bolsher, the warehouseman was of the same opinion, and he identified one of the

had only given them £3 on account. She subsequently stated that she had given £8 for the cotton. She and Fernie were then apprehended. The latter said he gave Toman

bags found at Fernie's as the property of his employers. - Mr Armstrong, one of the prosecutors, spoke to the cotton produced being similar to the Sicilian cotton stored upon their premises, brought from Catania [Sicily] in the steamer *Livorno*. -The prisoners were committed for trial.

Cotton bales from the United States being unloaded and stored in warehouses at Liverpool docks.

THE LIVERPOOL MERCURY
24th December 1863

A MARINE STORE DEALER IN TROUBLE- Matthew Butler-Murphy marine-store dealer, Vauxhall-road was charged with having been in possession about 1cwt. of cotton for which he could not satisfactorily account. Detectives Marsden and Fitzsimmons apprehended the prisoner at his store in Vauxhall-road that morning, and Marsden told

him that he charged him with being in illegal possession of about 1cwt. of cotton which they had found at his store in Worfield-street. Murphy made the reply, "I know nothing about those stores. I gave them away about a couple of weeks ago. The cotton does not belong to me and I know nothing about the stores". It appears that on Monday last, Marsden found the cotton at the stores in question and locked up the young man who was in charge of the stores. When the latter was brought before court the next day, Mr. Cobb [solicitor] defended him, and urged that he was not the person to be apprehended, but that his master should be charged. The prisoner was consequently discharged and Murphy was taken into custody.

Mr Cobb now appeared for him and in reply to him the former said that he did not know that Murphy paid the rent, but he knew that he was the tenant of the store in question. A young man named Alan Nichol, in the service of Mr. Fox, cotton broker, the owner of the stores, said the name of the tenant was Thomas Branagan, and that he had been the tenant for the last four months. Marsden said the prisoner's wife's maiden name was Branagan, and Thomas Branagan was at sea. The magistrate said the case was quite clear, and he could not allow a colourable tenancy like this to interfere with the ends of justice. The prisoner had acted as master of the place within four months, and he (his worship) would look upon him as it the tenant. It was stated that the prisoner had been in custody previously respecting some wool, but he was discharged. The magistrate ordered him to pay a fine of £6 plus costs for not accounting telling him that if he was again brought up on a similar charge the punishment would be absolute imprisonment. The fine was paid.

Vauxhall Road, 1869 (WG Herdman). **Source:** *www.Liverpoolpicturebook.com*

CHAPTER 6

1864

THE DAILY POST
15th January 1864

DISHONEST DOMESTICS. — Eliza, Catherine, Mary Ann and Ellen Dalton, four young women, sisters, were placed in the dock charged under the following circumstances: The prisoner Eliza Dalton was servant at the shop of Mr. Shannon, draper, Scotland-road, who has also a millinery establishment on the opposite side the street. She was given in charge to Detective Marsden on Monday night, and a quantity of property, consisting of velvet, feathers flowers, &c., to the value of about £2 having been found in her box, she acknowledged having taken them from the millinery establishment, which was under the management of Miss Jane Shannon. She was brought on Tuesday last, and remanded for further inquiry.

Since then Marsden went to 26, Blackfield-terrace, Stanley-road, Mr. Shannon's private residence, where the prisoner Catherine was servant, and found in her possession a hat, which Miss Shannon identified having been taken from her shop. In an old glove belonging to the prisoner the officer found a sovereign, which the prisoner first said had been given to her by her uncle when she was leaving Dublin. Subsequently she said that she very sorry, and that the hat was taken from a line in the shop, and she had found the sovereign under the bed. Marsden then took the prisoner into custody, and went to house in Gerard-street, in a room of which he found the other two prisoners, Mary Ann and Ellen, working at boot-binding. He found there several bonnets, caps, and other articles which had been stolen from Mr. Shannon's shop, and given to Mary Ann and Ellen by their sisters, who were in Mr. Shannon's service. The officer then locked them up in the Bridewell.

The prisoners Mary Ann and Ellen Dalton were discharged, Mr. Raffles saying that though the case against them was very suspicious, there was a doubt; and he would give them the benefit of it. Catherine Dalton was remanded for seven days, and the other prisoner, Eliza, was ordered to be imprisoned for three months.

Gerard Street off Scotland Road.

Gerard Street c.1870.

THE LIVERPOOL MERCURY
31st March 1864

THE MURDEROUS ATTACK BY THE MATE OF A SHIP.—George Mellor, the mate of the ship Vancouver, charged with committing a murderous assault upon Daniel Fairfield, a seaman belonging to that vessel, under circumstances detailed at length in the *Mercury*, was brought before the stipendiary magistrate at the police court yesterday. Detective Marsden stated that Mellor surrendered himself that morning, and when charged with the offence replied, "I did do it, and I shall be able to explain the cause of my doing it." The officer asked that the prisoner might be remanded for seven days. The injured man was not in a very dangerous state, but he would not be able to appear in court yet. Mr. Bremner, who appeared on behalf of the prisoner, said he thought they had a complete answer to the case. He did not oppose a remand, but asked the magistrate to admit Mellor to bail. His worship consented to do so on Mellor finding two sureties in £20 each. The case was remanded for seven days, and, the required bail being procured, the prisoner was liberated.

On further reading into this case, it seems that ship's mate George Mellor had previously threatened to kill his fellow crewman Daniel Fairfield. In this incident, he attacked Fairfield with an axe causing a number of severe injuries. Fairfield eventually recovered, however there is no record of George Mellor ever being charged with this assault. Exactly why this happened is unclear, but may reveal the somewhat arbitrary nature of the judicial system at this time.

THE DAILY POST
22nd April 1864

A SHIP'S STEWARD CHARGED WITH POCKET PICKING. - George Bremer, the young man who was remanded on the 15th instant on a charge of having stolen a quantity of silk pocket handkerchiefs and purses, found in his possession when apprehended by detective officer Marsden, at the Zoological Gardens, on Good Friday, was again brought up. Mr Cobb, who appeared for the prisoner, said his client would plead guilty. He was most respectably connected, and this was the first time he had offended. He had been employed by Messrs. Carver and Co. and others in the town in positions of trust, and hitherto had conducted himself with strict honesty and propriety. He had been four voyages in the Persia and two to the Arabia as second steward. This would be such a lesson to him as he would never forget, and it was the intentions of his friends to send him out of the country as soon as his was liberated. -Witnesses to character having been called, Mr Raffles said he would rather not convict the prisoner, and he thought the offence was committed under some unaccountable impulse, but he would remand him until he was assured that some provision would be made for sending him away. The prisoner was accordingly again remanded for seven days.

This particular case is important as it highlights how the concept of 'respectability' would have a bearing on how those committing crimes were treated before the law. Here George Bremer is caught stealing handkerchiefs and purses but somehow avoids prosecution on account of his being 'most respectably connected'. Mr Raffles decides that Bremer had suffered from some sort of mental aberration when he committed theft and would therefore allow Bremer to be spirited out of the country by his friends. It is difficult not to draw comparisons between this case and that of mill workers James Kenzie and Patrick Foy (17th July 1862) who were jailed for stealing four bags of rice flour (Chapter 4).

Liverpool Zoological Gardens on West Derby Road. Detective Marsden apprehended pickpocket George Bremer here on Good Friday 1864.

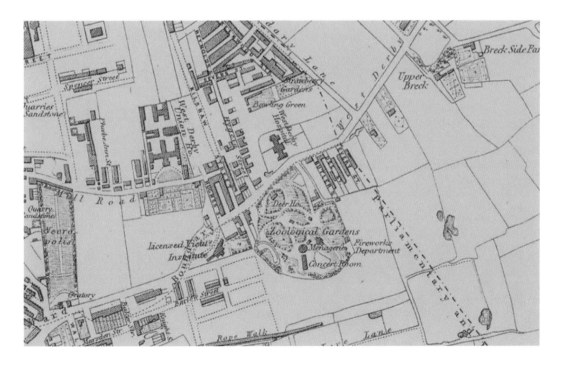

THE HULL ADVERTISER
2nd July 1864

DARING OUTRAGE AND GAROTTE ROBBERY IN LIVERPOOL.—At the police-court, on Tuesday, three men, named respectively John Macdonald, David Atheron, and John Powell, were charged with having murderously assaulted William Lawrene, and robbed him of his gold watch, a sum of money, and other property. From the evidence it appeared that about eleven o'clock on the night of the 9th inst., the prosecutor was in Clarence-street, when he was suddenly seized from behind, was knocked down, nearly choked, and had his head almost twisted off, His assailants, having by this process rendered the prosecutor insensible, robbed him of his watch, a sum of money, and other property, with which, at the time, they made clear off. Subsequently they were apprehended by Detective Marsden, and after hearing the evidence, Mr. Raffles committed the prisoners for trial at the assizes.

JOHN O'GROATS JOURNAL - WICK
7th July 1864

MURDEROUS GAROTTE ROBBERY IN LIVERPOOL.- On the night of the 9th, about 11 o'clock, the prosecutor was in Clarence Street, on his way home, when he was suddenly seized from behind, knocked down, and nearly chocked. His assailants then robbed him of his watch, with other property, and some money. Sometime afterwards a detective officer, named Marsden, heard some conversation in a public house in Scotland Road, and in consequence of what he heard, he arrested three persons on suspicion of having committed some depredation, and after he had secured them at the station house, a report of the robbery and outrage was made by the prosecutor, and on the prisoners being placed amongst a number of men. Lawrence at once identified them as the parties who had robbed and nearly killed him. The prisoners were committed for trial at the Assizes.

The Lawrence case (above) gives us an intriguing glimpse into Detective Marsden's methods of crime detection. He overhears a conversation between criminals in a pub on Scotland Road, which shows that he is using surveillance and covert methods to gather evidence. Was he in disguise and posing as a customer when he gleaned this piece of information?

Clarence Street. William Lawrence was garrotted and robbed here in 1864. Source:www.liverpoolpicturebook.com

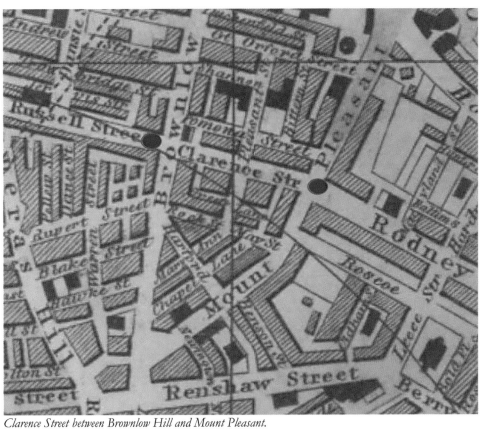

Clarence Street between Brownlow Hill and Mount Pleasant.

DANGEROUS ASSAULT UPON A WIFE.— A middle-aged man named Henry Townrow, a painter in the employ of Messrs. Seaton and Boggs, upholsterers, Bold-street, and residing in No. 1 Court, Juvenal-place, was brought charged with having committed a serious assault upon his wife, about a fortnight since. The prisoner had not been apprehended until Thursday night, when he was taken into custody at his own house by Detective Marsden. A certificate was now read from Mr. Rae, house surgeon at St. Anne's Dispensary, to the effect that the prisoner's wife was in a dying state. The wife had stated to the police that her husband had caused her injuries by leaning upon her side and striking her about the head. The prisoner did not deny having committed the assault but said he had been greatly provoked. On Saturday night he had given his wife 31s, and when he went home on Sunday at noon there was no dinner for him, and his wife was in beastly state of intoxication by the evening of the same day.—The officer stated that the prisoner's employers gave him a good character. —Mr. Raffles observed that the prisoner appeared to have received great provocation and hoped for the prisoner's sake that his wife would get better. He could not admit him bail, however, while the woman was in such a dangerous condition, and he would be remanded for seven days.

The Townrow case above highlights the enormous problem of domestic violence during this era. As Archer (2011) explains, in order to get any kind of justice: "a battered woman had to be able to prove her character was good and her behaviour temperate, obedient and modest." Therefore, it was not unusual for a man to be arrested for assaulting his wife, only to be discharged when it was found that he had been provoked because she was considered to be a drunk, lazy or a bad housekeeper. Macilwee (2011) tells us that even the Chaplain of Walton Gaol believed that men were 'provoked' into beating their wives and suggested that the women of Liverpool were worse than the men in terms of intemperate and disorderly behaviour. He asked who could blame decent, law-abiding husbands raising their hands to such a women? During the nineteenth century, many in authority viewed domestic violence as a problem of the lower classes. The effects of alcohol, a lack of education and 'an innate brutality' were thought to be the root cause.

In addition, police at this time considered domestic violence to be somewhat out of their remit. If a woman was subject to an unprovoked attack by her husband, her male relatives (such as her father or brothers) were expected to step in and 'sort him out'. Police were also reluctant to become involved because, in order to enter a private dwelling to investigate a domestic incident, a warrant would have to be issued by a magistrate. The necessity of obtaining such a warrant often caused police officers to be apathetic in their response to reports of intermarital violence. Neighbours, although aware that domestic violence was happening close by, rarely interfered. Some may have believed it was a husband's right to beat his wife (and children), others may have simply been too afraid to risk turning that violence toward themselves and therefore chose to turn a blind eye.

A REAL HARD CASE.

(THE ROUGH'S LAST WRONG.)

Liverpool Ruffian. "'ERE'S A GO!—A MAN 'ANGED FOR KICKIN' HIS WIFE TO DEATH! I SHALL 'AVE TO TAKE MY BOOTS OFF!"

Punch Magazine 1875

'The Drunkard's Children'. G. Cruikshank, 1857.

THE LIVERPOOL MERCURY
24th September 1864

A MOTHER CHARGED WITH NEGLECTING HER CHILDREN. -Elizabeth Thompson, the woman charged with neglecting her children and making one of them drunk, was again brought up. On the 16th instant the prisoner was found by a policeman in Scotland-road in a state of intoxication, having in her arms an infant in a filthy condition and which was found to be in consumption. One of her daughters, seven years old, was lying at her feet upon the pavement "insensibly drunk". -Detective Marsden said he had, as directed, made enquiries respecting the prisoner, and found that she was the wife of a hard-working man, employed as a porter at the Wapping Dock, and living at No. 2 Court, Trueman-street. She was in the habit of "going on the spree" for a week together, leaving her children with no one to take care of them. One of the children, a delicate looking little girl, said she was left to take care of her brothers and sisters. The prisoner's husband was called into the witness-box and stated that he believed his wife behaved well to their family and gave them plenty to eat. In defence the prisoner said she left home for some days because her husband had quarrelled with her. Whilst she was in a public house having some drink with a woman whom she knew, the child who was found drunk took up her glass and drank the liquor it contained. As soon as she saw the infant was ill she was going to the druggist's to get something for it, and the policeman then took her into custody. Mr. Preston told her she had very nearly brought herself within the meshes of the law. He cautioned her as to her future conduct. She might new be discharged, but if brought there again she might find herself placed in a very different position.

90

Elizabeth Thompson's case was not unusual. During the nineteenth century children were often given alcohol by their parents. Babies were given alcohol to treat colic (in gripe water) and older children were given it to make them sleep. A further problem involving alcohol within families was the 'overlaying' of children. In Liverpool alone, between 1st July 1861 and 30th June 1862, eighty-one babies were accidentally smothered or 'overlaid' after being taken to sleep in their parents bed during the night. Most deaths occurred on Saturday nights and Sunday mornings when parents, after drinking alcohol, took the baby into bed between them. At some time during the night, the baby would be suffocated by one of the parents rolling on top of it while intoxicated. The damaged caused by alcohol and its effects on the family and children was a cause of serious concern for magistrates, police, churchmen and journalists across the country during the nineteenth century. Shimmin (1870) was particularly scathing of drunken parents. He describes seeing a woman emerge from a public house after hours of drinking to find her child waiting outside for her:

"Look by the curb-stone. See that little creature with curly hair, and its face and legs so caked with dirt that the flesh is not discernible. Hear how piteously it cries... the little hands, fresh from the gutter, are pressed against it eyes as it strives to cross the street and reach its mother."

Fetching beer from the pub. Scotland Road, late nineteenth century. (Liverpool Records Office, Liverpool Libraries)

A street urchin makes money by singing for customers in a Liverpool pub.

Children were often sent to public houses with bottles and jugs to bring back beer for their parents. © *Liverpool Records Office, Liverpool Libraries.*

CHAPTER 7

1865

THE LIVERPOOL MAIL
4th March 1865

ROBBERY FROM A PUBLIC HOUSE - Yesterday, at the Police Court, before Mr. Mills, James Scully, a well-known thief and a woman named Bridget McMullen, were brought up in custody, on the charge of having feloniously entered the dwelling-house of James Murphy, licensed victualler, in Adlington-street, and stolen there from a quantity of spirits and wearing apparel, to the value of about £6 10s. On the night of the first inst. Mr Murphy when to bed about 10 o'clock having to get up to get up early in the morning. On Murphy coming downstairs the following morning, about half past five o'clock, he found the front window open and the back door unfastened. He called his wife and on an examination of the premises being made, it was found that a gallon of brandy, a gallon of rum, two quart pewter measures, and a quantity of wearing apparel altogether of the value about £6 10s, had been stolen. The same forenoon information of the robbery was given to detective-officers Marsden and Fitzsimmons, and they, in consequence of the information they had received, went to a house kept by the female prisoner, No. 16 Court, Adlington-street, where they found the prisoner Scully drinking rum. McCullen was also there, and on seeing the officers, she made a rush with a pot mug full of rum, which she attempted to throw into a tub of water. On the chimney-piece there was a bottle of rum, and upstairs under a bed in room occupied by Scully, the officers found a coat and quantity of other wearing apparel stolen from the house of Mr Murphy; in the cellar they also found a gallon of brandy, and a can containing a quart of rum. The prisoners, in answer to the officers, said they knew nothing the property. The female prisoner said to Scully, "0 Jemmy, what made you bring them here." The above facts having been proved in evidence, the prisoners were committed for trial.

Adlington Street where Detectives Marsden and Fitzsimmons apprehended Scully and McMullen.

Robert Marsden and the Street Arabs of Liverpool

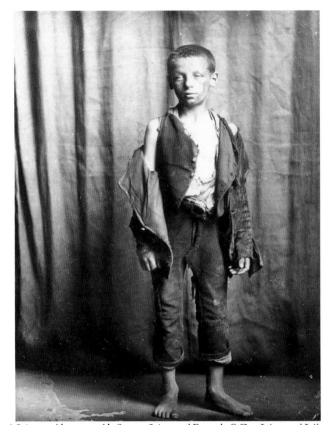

A Liverpool 'street arab'. Source: Liverpool Records Office, Liverpool Libraries

In August 1865 the Liverpool Daily Post received a letter from an anonymous author. The writer of the letter commends the action taken by Detective Robert Marsden and magistrate Mr Raffles in their efforts to help some of Liverpool's street children (known locally as 'street arabs'). It is thought that during the mid-nineteenth century, Liverpool was home to some 25,000 street children. These children were often orphaned, abandoned, runaways or those who were described as 'beyond the control of their parents'. They were found in large groups living in derelict buildings, alleyways and in the streets around the docks.

Liverpool's most famous 'street arab' was the character 'Heathcliff' in Emily Bronte's *Wuthering Heights*. Shortly before writing her novel in 1846, Emily's brother Branwell had visited Liverpool and on his return told her about the thousands of children he had seen living on the streets of the town. These descriptions may have given her the idea for Heathcliff, who when he is found on the streets of Liverpool is described as being "a dirty, ragged, black-haired child... starving and houseless... not a soul knew to whom [he] belonged." Street children who were caught committing crimes (usually stealing food, begging and pickpocketing) appeared in the Liverpool Police Court on a daily basis. When convicted, girls would be sent to a house of correction, or later the Industrial School in Kirkdale. Boys would be whipped or birched. Repeat offenders would be sent to the juvenile reformatory ships *Akbar* and *Clarence*, which were anchored in the River Mersey. The writer of the letter argues that reformatory ships brutalised, hardened and degraded these boys even further and that Detective Marsden and Magistrate Raffles had adopted a different strategy which produced far better results.

THE STREET ARABS OF LIVERPOOL AND HOW TO TREAT THEM. The following letter has been addressed to the 'Liverpool Daily Post':-

Sir, some time ago, in the discharge of a public duty, you had to make a few observations with reference to unfortunate boys who are conned on board the reformatory ship *Clarence.* Those observations, although strong, were considered, even by the most ardent admirers of the system, at least just, and the following case is perhaps the strongest illustration of your views that could be found to sustain what you then advanced.

Some eight or nine months ago Detective Officer Marsden, of this town, picked up one of these juvenile Arabs in Scotland Road. The lad, whose name is Peter McQuiggan, was in a most deplorable condition of destitution; the officer, with a kind-heartedness worthy of imitation, took the outcast boy for shelter to the station-house, and on making some inquiry he found that the boy had already suffered some short term of imprisonment for a slight offence. He also discovered that there was much natural shrewdness (miscalled by some persons 'intelligence') about the boy, and that this, put into a proper training channel, might lead to gratifying results. The lad expressed a wish for a sea life, and officer Marsden interested himself with the worthy stipendiary magistrate [Mr Raffles] and other gentlemen, and procured the unfortunate youth, not only some clothes but also a ship on which he went on a long voyage, receiving a few shillings a month for his services on board the vessel.

The boy had passed from the memory of his benefactor; but, on Friday last, a fine sailor-like youth, well dressed and with a manly independent air about him, ran up to the officer in the street, caught him affectionately by the hand exclaiming, "Oh, father! I was looking for you to return you my thanks." This was the Arab of some nine months before — but how changed! Well fed, well clothed, he stood before his benefactor in all the pride of juvenile independence. The rest is easily told. The boy had saved his wages, and added to them by some gratuities, which had been given to him for good conduct, and he came to lodge the amount with the man who was more than a father (as he called him) to him. He also informed the officer that he had got a better ship and larger wages, and that fearing any accident might happen to his money, he had come to lodge it for safe keeping, as he would require it for the purpose of new clothes on his next voyage, which would commence in a week.

The only comment necessary on this narrative is a moral that may fairly be drawn from it. Had this boy been left on the streets he would, almost inevitably, have been driven to steal for his support, and the next scene would have been the reformatory ship. Now, suppose that he had learned to "bend, reef, end steer" on board the *Clarence,* would he not have gone on board a merchant ship with a sense of degradation about him? And no matter how prudent his conduct in later life might be, would he ever possess that manly, independent, self-reliant spirit and character of little Peter McQuiggan, the Street Arab of Liverpool, who was reclaimed by a kind-hearted police-officer, and who may become a good and respectable member of society in place of a returned convict, end all this because the right end of the wedge was used in the first instance? R.

THE PORCUPINE
12th December 1868

Many boys who are brought before Mr Raffles, wish to go to sea, and if he finds, on the inquiry of an officer - he generally deputes to Mr Robert Marsden, who is indeed one of the most intelligent of the twelve under the superintendence of Mr L Kehoe - that the lad bears a good character, he not only forwards his inclination, but at his own expense procures him an outfit of clothes. Then his kindness is ably seconded by Mr Joseph Jenkins, the Superintendent of the Local Marine Board, who procures a ship for the boy. In this way we have seen many a lad rescued; and what is still more pleasing, there are a few weeks that pass without some fine, manly, well-dressed boys presenting themselves before his worship and tendering him heartfelt thanks for having saved them from destruction. The other day a stout sailor lad was presented to Mr Raffles as we stood by. The lad had been snatched from crime, clothed and got off to sea through the good offices of the magistrate. He had been fifteen months away, and, from a puny starveling, had become a hardy looking young sailor. It would be difficult to say which looked the most delighted, the boy or he who had been instrumental in making him what he was. The scene was suggestive and a very pleasant one to look upon.

© Liverpool Records Office, Liverpool Libraries.

"Small mites some of them little more than babies... woeful little specimens of humanity encrusted with filth and barely covered in rags are brought [before the court] charged with begging and burglary." (The Liverpool Review)

"at the door of every gin shop... stood puny young shivering children, in filth and tatters. 'Please give me a penny' or 'please buy a box of matches', uttered in a drawl, first calls attention to these sorrowful and pitiful objects". (Shimmin, 1862)

All pictures: © Liverpool Records Office, Liverpool Libraries.

CHARGE OF MURDER AND ATTEMPT TO MURDER IN LIVERPOOL. At the Police Court, yesterday, a young man named Daniel McKenna, who has for some time past been employed as "lofter up" at Mr. Jack's foundry, Victoria Road, was brought before Mr. Raffles, stipendiary magistrate, charged with having murdered William McManus, a fireman on board the steamship *Helvetia*, and who resided, when at home, in Menai-terrace, Menai-street, off Athol-street. He was also charged with attempting to murder John Grady, a labourer, who lives with his friends in Athol-street. Mr. Superintendent Kehoe, in opening the case, intimated that he intended to offer merely sufficient evidence to justify the remand he applied for. When the magistrate had heard the evidence he (Mr. Kehoe) thought his worship would be of opinion that it was a case of murder and not of aggravated manslaughter. In addition to killing the unfortunate man McManus, the prisoner had barely escaped sending another man into eternity. When pursuing the deceased, a man named John Grady interfered, and the prisoner stabbed him in the abdomen, and Grady was so much injured that he was unable to attend the court that day.

Detective Marsden was then called. He stated that about eleven o'clock on Sunday night he and Detective Fitzsimmons were sent to Athol-Street, in consequence of information which had been received at the Central Police Office. About a quarter-past six o'clock that morning they apprehended the prisoner in the cellar of a house in Barmouth-street, off Athol-street. He had fresh clothes on, and witness [Marsden] told him he wanted the clothes he had on Saturday night. The prisoner's mother said they were covered with filth. By the witness's direction the prisoner put them on and was brought out of the cellar. Witness then inquired of him if he knew who he and Fitzsimmons were, and on his stating he did not, the witness told him they were detectives. As they were going towards the Police Office, and before the officers made any charge against him, said, "I got into a fearful row last night close to a public house near the railway arch. I became insensible all once, and I don't know what I've done." He was quite sober then. At the Police Office he was placed amongst number of other men and once identified by four witnesses. He (Marsden) then charged him with having caused the death of a man named McManus and also with stabbing a man named Grady. The prisoner replied, "I don't know anything all about it. I never used a knife. I would in bed about that time," referring to nine o'clock on Sunday night.

A young man named William Nicholson stated that between eight and nine o'clock on Sunday night he was in the "snug" of Bell's public house. Boundary-street, Kirkdale, in company with the deceased, Mary McManus, and several other persons. Whilst they were sitting in the snug the prisoner entered. He was to all appearance quite sober. Witness thought the deceased seemed to know who the prisoner was. McKenna asked if Daniel Close was there, and the deceased pointed him out as sitting at the bottom of the table. The prisoner appeared to be vexed about something, and some words took place between him and Close, when witness told him that if he struck the latter he must strike witness. McKenna, however, struck at Close, and then witness struck at him. Deceased then got up and told the prisoner he should not come there to make a disturbance and turned him out of the snug.

McKenna afterwards stood outside the room, near the counter, and in ten minutes after the quarrel occurred the whole party, including the deceased and witness, left the house together. The prisoner went out before them, and when witness got into the street he saw McKenna rush up to the deceased and strike him in the lower part of the abdomen. The deceased cried out that he was "stoved" or "murdered."

Witness did not see any knife in the hand of McKenna. The latter bolted off after he had struck the deceased, and witness ran after him, but he slipped and fell, and the prisoner made his escape. So far as he could see, McManus had given McKenna no provocation. Shortly after the prisoner ran away witness saw McManus lying dead at the house of Dr. Costine, in Athol-street.

Mr. Kehoe said the unfortunate man was taken to the house of Dr. Costine directly after he was stabbed and died a few minutes subsequently. Mr. Kehoe also said he did not know whether the man Grady would recover. The Magistrate considered this evidence quite sufficient for a remand, and the prisoner was remanded accordingly. He seemed to be sensible of the serious position in which he was placed. The 'Helvetia' arrived in this port on Sunday, and the hapless man McManus had only been at home a few hours when he lost his life.

Illustrated Police News, 21st August 1869

CHAPTER 8

1866

THE LIVERPOOL MERCURY
7th MARCH 1866

HOUSEBREAKING BY BOYS -Two boys. named John Jones and Thomas Sandon were brought up on remand charged with breaking into the shop of Mr. Christopher Doherty, pawnbroker, Marybone, and stealing wearing apparel and other goods, together of the value of between £4 and £5; and two women named Alice Eaves and Sarah Gilchrist were charged with receiving the property, or a portion of it, knowing it to be stolen. Mr. Campbell defended Gilchrist. On the night of the 25th of January. John Robertson, assistant to the prosecutor, closed the shop as usual, and left all apparently secure. There is a spring lock to the door in the lobby of the house communicating with the shop. This door was closed when the assistant left. Several persons slept upon the premises. The next morning Robertson found that the door communicating with the lobby had been forced open, an entrance gained thus to the shop, and the property referred to carried off. The shop seemed to have been completely ransacked and was in great disorder. The evidence given at former hearings was repeated, it being proved that the stolen goods were traced to the possession of the male prisoners, that the women had been in communication with the boys, and had pledged, or caused to be pledged some of the stolen property. All the prisoners were committed for trial at the sessions. -The boys were further charged with breaking into the shop of Mr Bridson, pawnbroker, at the corner of Benlodi-street, Scotland-road, and stealing wearing apparel worth £7 nearly the whole of which had been recovered by Detectives Marsden and Fitzsimmons, the two officers in the case. The women were also charged with feloniously receiving the goods in this instance. The prisoners were all committed for trial.

The training ship 'Akbar' anchored in the Mersey. This was a gaol for juvenile offenders. It was argued they would benefit from being taught the skills and discipline of life at sea.

At the Lancaster Assizes on 6th April 1866 Sarah Gilchrist, John Jones, Thomas Sandon and Alice Eaves were all charged with shop breaking. Sarah Gilchrist is sentenced to two years in prison. John Jones twelve months in prison. Thomas Sandon fourteen days in prison and then to be sent to the Liverpool 'Akbar' Reformatory ship for 5 years. Alice Eaves was found not guilty.

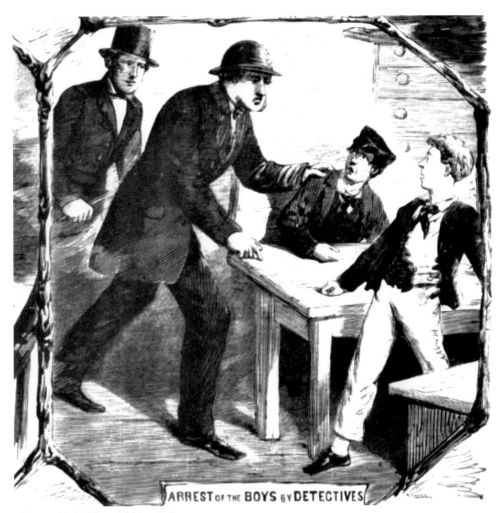

Illustrated Police News, 9th May 1869

Detective Marsden And Liverpool's Infamous Reid Murder Case of 1866

In December 1862, a man named Robert Reid stabbed and killed his wife Ann at their home on Thurlow Street (later renamed Myrtle Street) Liverpool. Reid immediately disappeared and for nearly four years remained at large. For a number of decades, New York and Liverpool police had worked closely together, exchanging information about offenders fleeing and entering the United States and Britain through the ports of New York and Liverpool. In July 1866, police in Brooklyn arrested a man for being drunk and disorderly. He matched the description of Robert Reid. New York police wrote to their colleagues in Liverpool City Police who then made arrangements to positively identify the suspect and return him to Britain. The following is an excerpt from the minutes of the acting Superintendent to the Liverpool Watch Committee for July 1866. In these it is proposed that a police officer should take Mary Rogers (who had witnessed Ann Reid's murder) to New York in order to identify the suspect Robert Reid. In the event that a confirmed identification was made, the police officer would then extradite Robert Reid back to Liverpool to be tried for Ann Reid's murder. The police officer chosen to travel to New York with the murder witness was Robert Marsden.

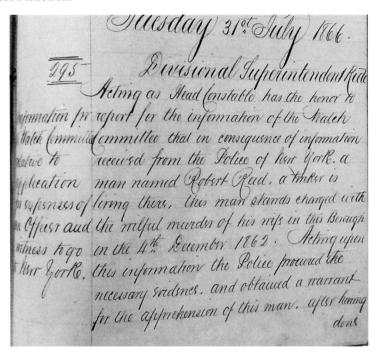

Transcription: *Tuesday 31st July 1866. Application for the expenses of a Police officer and witness to go to New York. - Divisional Superintendent Ride acting as Head Constable has the honor to report for the information of the Watch Committee that in consequence of information received from the Police of New York, a man named Robert Reid, a tinker, is living there. This man stands charged with the wilful murder of his wife in this Borough on the 4th December 1862. Acting upon this information the Police provided the necessary evidences, and obtained a warrant for the apprehension of this man. After having done so, the case was submitted to the authorities in London by his Worship the Mayor, and a communication has been received from the Home Office which is now in the Town Hall directing that an Officer be sent to execute the warrant, and that all reasonable expenses will be paid by the Government. It is proposed to send the Officer and his witness by tomorrow's steamer. This day Mr Superintendent Kehoe and the Deputy Town Clerk made application to the Borough Treasurer for £150, to pay all reasonable expenses in going to New York and returning. Mr Tweedie refused to advance any money for such purposes. It may be the pleasure of the Watch Committee to make such order under the advice of their Law Clerk as they think proper. It is important for the interests of justice that no further delay should take place.*

On 2nd August 1866, Detective Marsden and murder witness Mary Rogers boarded the paddle steamer *Etna* at Princes Landing Stage, Liverpool and made the eight-day crossing to New York City, arriving on 10th August. Manhattan in August would have a place of stifling heat, ramshackle landing stages, densely packed tenements and masses of immigrants from all over the world. Robert Marsden would have been grateful for the assistance that was given to him by his colleagues in the New York Police Department.

BROADWATERS BUCKINGHAMSHIRE ADVERTISER AND UXBRIDGE JOURNAL
14th August 1866

MURDER OF MRS REED IN 1862. APPREHENSION OF THE MURDERER IN AMERICA. Sometime towards the end of 1862 a most diabolical murder was perpetrated in Richmond Row, Liverpool, the victim of the foul deed being Mrs Reed, the wife of a tinplate worker. Immediately after the murder, the husband of the murdered woman disappeared, and, notwithstanding the endeavours of the police to trace him, he managed to keep out of the way until within the last few weeks, when he fell into the hands of the United States authorities. Reed, it appears, who was well known to the Liverpool police, carried on a comfortable business in Richmond Row; but, in consequence of irregularities on his part, there were often family quarrels in which Reed once or twice threatened to "do" for his wife. It was on a Saturday night, daring the period mentioned above, that Reid came home apparently dissatisfied about something, and not finding Mrs. Reed at home, he ascertained that she was at a neighbour's house and sent for her. She returned home in about a quarter of an hour, and from about that time (about half-past eleven at night) until she was found in a dying state nothing was seen or heard of her or her husband. When found by some neighbours, she had a deep and fatal wound in her left ribs, and all the evidence collected showed clearly that her husband was the murderer. However, after being free of upwards of three years, he has been secured, and Detective Marsden, of the Liverpool police force, has just left Liverpool for New York in the steamer the Etna, the same vessel that brought Muller to Liverpool from America. for the purpose of bringing Reed back to the scene of his wife's murder.

Steam ship 'Etna' aboard which Detective Marsden travelled to New York with murder witness Mary Rogers. Here it is depicted a number of years later being damaged in a storm.

THE SCOTSMAN
3rd September 1866

APPREHENSION OF A MAN FOR MURDER COMMITTED NEARLY FOUR YEARS AGO. —On the 4th December 1862, a woman named Reid, the wife of a tinker living in Thurlow Street, Liverpool, was murdered by her husband. He knocked her down, kicked her, and stabbed her with a knife, which he afterwards threw into a sewer. The murderer made his escape and succeeded in evading apprehension until the 20th ultimo. Intimation was given to the Liverpool police that Reid was in New York, and Marsden, one of the Liverpool detectives was sent over there. Yesterday, a letter dated "New York, 20th August," was received by Superintendent Kehoe, head of the Liverpool detective force, from Marsden, stating that he arrived at New York on 10th. He received, the assistance of the New York police, and on Saturday the 18th discovered that Reid was conned in Brooklyn Gaol for ten days, for having been drunk and disorderly. After a communication with the British Consul, Reid was given into the custody of the English officer, who lodged him in a New York jail for safety until the necessary papers warranting his transmission to Liverpool are received from Washington. Mary Rogers, the woman who saw Reid stab his wife and throw the knife into the sewer (who was taken to New York by Marsden to identify Reid) recognised Reid immediately upon seeing him. Reid does not deny the charge made against him. Marsden informs Mr Kehoe that he proposes sailing with the prisoner on the *'City of London'* which is due in Liverpool on Wednesday next.

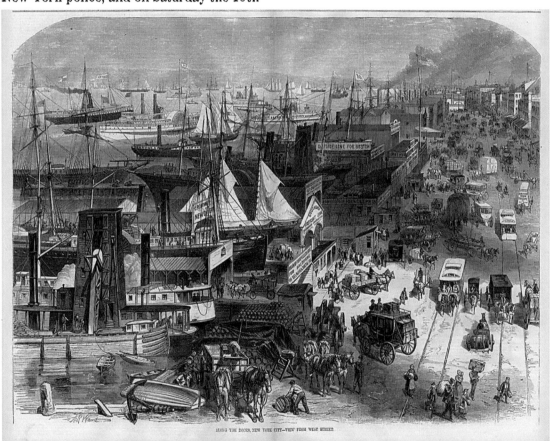

New York docks as Detective Marsden would have seen them when he disembarked with murder witness Mary Rogers in August 1866.

28th Precinct police station and gaol in modern day Harlem, New York City. Marsden held Robert Reid here whilst waiting for extradition papers to arrive from Washington DC.

Whilst the townspeople of Liverpool awaited the return of fugitive Robert Reid, newspapers began to print daily reports on the circumstances surrounding Ann Reid's murder four years previously. In the following article, Robert Reid's criminal past and the events leading up to his wife's death are described in detail.

THE LIVERPOOL DAILY POST
3rd September 1866

On Wednesday night, the 4th December, 1862, a man named Robert Reid, who occupied No. 7 Cellar, Lower Myrtle-street, off Thurlow Street, murdered his wife, Ann Reid, in most craven and unprovoked manner. Reid was an itinerant tinker, and at one period of his life had been soldier, but it would seem that the discipline and precision of military life ill afforded with his reckless and ungovernable nature, for, in order obtain discharge without serving his full term service, he resorted to self-mutilation and cut off two of his fingers. Thurlow Street and its neighbourhood is the home of some of the most lawless characters in Liverpool, but even amongst ruffianism hereabout located, Reid had a reputation for coarse brutality and uncontrollable impulse, and that it was libel may be concluded from the circumstances of the murder. On the night already named, Ann Reid, and a woman of the name of Mary Rogers, were sitting conversing in the cellar when Reid and his son entered. To all appearances he was in a genial and convivial mood, for he began singing, and after going through a song called upon his wife to sing. She obeyed his request. The theme of her song did not please him, and he ordered her to stop; but she was not so willing to obey the second request as she had been to obey the first, and therefore continued her song. This was more than Reid's temper could bear, and he seized his wife by the hair of the head and dragged her across the cellar. The woman Rogers expostulated with him upon his brutality, and he then stopped. Mrs. Reid got up, walked to the chimney corner, and sat down, resting her head upon her shoulder. Apparently she was conscious, and did not speak. A moment or two later Mrs. Rogers noticed blood owing from under her left arm and she called the attention of Reid to it. Thereupon he turned to his son, and said, "Come on, Johnny," and left the cellar. Mrs. Rogers followed him and raised a cry of "Murder." As he went out of the cellar a girl named Ada saw him with a bloodstained knife in his band and observed him go to a sewer in the street and throw the knife through the grating. Meanwhile his wife, who had received two severe stabs in the upper part of the arm, severing the main artery, had bled to death.

Although the fact was at made known to the police, and the detective force put in motion, Read, notwithstanding the utmost precautionary measures being taken, made an effectual escape from Liverpool. The Government offered £100 reward for his detection, yet without avail. It was shrewdly suspected that he had fled to America, as he had before been a wanderer in the States. Acting upon that suspicion, the Detective Department of Liverpool opened a correspondence with that of New York respecting Reid. No immediate result followed, and a conviction gradually formed that failure of apprehension was inevitable. Four years lapsed away, and about four months since the New York detectives, by some fortuitous circumstance, fancied that they had seen the man Reid. Detective Inspector Farley, of New York, communicated with Detective Inspector Carlisle, of Liverpool, and the result was that search was made here for the witness who gave evidence to the coroner's inquisition on the body of the deceased woman. These persons were found and the woman Rogers who had been in the cellar on the night of the murder.

On the 2nd August last, Detective Marsden, accompanied by Mrs. Rogers, left Liverpool for New York in the steamer 'Etna' and arrived in New York on the 16th inst, and at once communicated with Kennedy, the Chief of the New York police, and this gentleman afforded Marsden every facility for bringing his excursion to successful issue. Reid had been honoured with the surveillance of the New York detectives for some months, and just prior to the arrival of Marsden at New York he found himself in the bands of the police as a drunk and disorderly person, and such he was committed to Brooklyn Gaol for a term of ten days. Here Marsden and Mrs. Rogers were introduced to him. Mrs. Rogers identified him the murderer Reid, and on being charged with that offence by Marsden he offered no denial. The necessary documents for his extradition were then completed, and, according to information received by the *'Java'* on Saturday, Marsden and his prisoner, and the woman Rogers, to have left New York in the *'City of London'*, which will be due in Liverpool on Wednesday.

Illustrated Police News 9 January 1869

THE THURLOW-STREET MURDER. APPREHENSION IN NEW YORK OF THE SUSPECTED MURDERER. The police authorities received on Saturday a communication informing them that Robert Reid, who is charged with murdering his wife, Ann Reid, in Liverpool, on the 4th of December, 1862, had been apprehended in New York. The crime which Reid is charged with committing, and the escape of the supposed murderer caused some sensation in the town. It was one of a series of terrible offences that were perpetrated in Liverpool within a short period. Almost in every instance the parties accused escaped, and although some of the crimes were committed in a crowded neighbourhood, and the persons implicated were well known, the police seemed for sometime to be at fault. Rewards were offered for information which would lead to the apprehension of the alleged murderers and when the slightest clue was obtained detectives were at once set to a work to follow it up. In most of the cases, however, nothing tangible was arrived at, and Liverpool became rather notorious for a long list of undiscovered murderers.

It was no doubt supposed by the public that the undetected criminals were beyond the reach of the authorities, and consequently they and their crimes were almost forgotten. But the police, although they may be baffled for a time, are generally on the alert for "information" which may put them on the track of offenders. America is often sought as a place of refuge by persons who flee from the old country to escape the consequence of their crimes. If, on arriving in the States they go "up the country," and remain silent as to their antecedents, their detection becomes almost an impossibility. Should they, however, take up their abode in New York or any of the large cities where the police organisation is effective, they are pretty sure to be discovered and brought to Justice.

An illustration of how "murder will out" is afforded in the apprehension of Reid. The accused, it will be recollected, was a tinker, and lived with his wife and child at No. 4, Lower Myrtle-street, Thurlow Street. in this town. On the night of Wednesday, the 4th of December 1862, the deceased woman, Ann Reid, and a female named Mary Rogers, were sitting in the cellar of the deceased's house, when the accused came in with his son. He commenced to sing and asked his wife to sing a song. She did so; but the song displeased Reid, who ordered her to stop singing. She would not do so, and he then got up and dragged her by the hair of the head to the doorstep. Rogers remonstrated with him, and he released his hold. His wife then walked from the door and lay down in a corner with her head and shoulder leaning against the wall, and the woman Rogers observed a stream of blood coming from under Mrs. Reid's arm. When the husband also noticed it he said to his son, "Come, Johnny," and left the cellar. Mrs.' Rogers ran after him and cried a "Murder," but he ran through an entry leading to Circus-street and made his escape. The injured woman died in about 20 minutes after her husband left.

A young woman named Mary Adams, who lived in a court opposite, was standing near the house at the time of the occurrence. She saw Reid coming out of the cellar, having in his hand a knife upon which was blood. He then went to a sewer in Myrtle-street and dropped the knife of through the grate. Subsequently Detective Fitzsimmons found the knife, which was a clasp one, in the sewer, and the girl Adams identified it as the one she had seen in Reid's hand. When Dr. Goodall Jones examined the deceased, he found two severe incised wounds on the upper and inner part of the left arm, and another on the shoulder. He was of the opinion that the stabs had been inflicted with a sharp instrument such as the knife found in the sewer.

Notwithstanding the exertions of the police and the offer of a reward of £100 for his apprehension, Reid escaped, and, it was believed at the time, made his way to America, where he had a some relatives, and where he had previously resided. A description of him was forwarded to the police in that country, but for some time nothing was heard of him. On the 4th August last Mr. Philip Farley an active officer in the Detective Department at New York, who has been in England and who has on many occasions afforded help to the English police, communicated to Detective Inspector Carlisle intimating that he had discovered a man in Brooklyn who answered in every particular the description of Reid. The necessary papers having been procured, Detective Marsden, accompanied by the woman Rogers, left Liverpool for New York. He arrived at the latter city on the 16th, and immediately put himself in communication with Mr. Kennedy, the Chief of the New York police, who directed Captain Dixon and Detective Eustace to assist the English officer in apprehending the man he wanted.. In a day or two they learned that their man was in safe keeping, having been sentenced to ten days' imprisonment in Brooklyn gaol for being drunk and disorderly. Marsden having received the necessary papers Reid was handed over to his custody. The woman Rogers identified him, and it is stated that he did not deny the charge. Marsden and his prisoner are expected to arrive in Liverpool on Wednesday by the *City of London*. The reward which was offered for Reid's apprehension will, we believe be given to the American police.

John Kennedy, Chief of the New York Police who assisted Detective Marsden in bringing Robert Reid to justice.

The paddle steamer 'City of London' which brought Detective Marsden, Robert Reid and Mary Rogers back to Liverpool from New York in 1866.

Princes Landing Stage, Liverpool where a 'crowd of roughs' waited Robert Reid to arrive from New York.

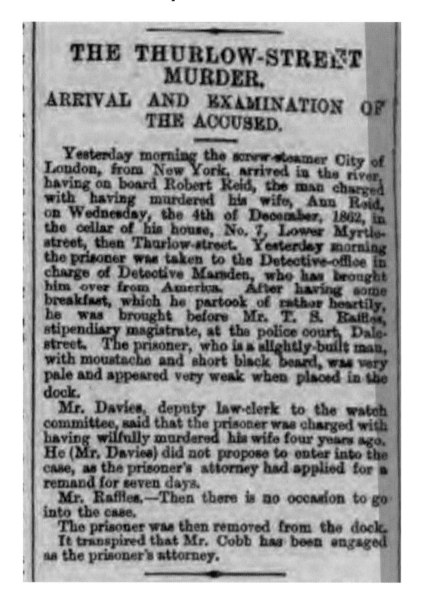

THE THURLOW-STREET MURDER.

ARRIVAL AND EXAMINATION OF THE ACCUSED.

Yesterday morning the screw-steamer City of London, from New York, arrived in the river, having on board Robert Reid, the man charged with having murdered his wife, Ann Reid, on Wednesday, the 4th of December, 1862, in the cellar of his house, No. 7, Lower Myrtle-street, then Thurlow-street. Yesterday morning the prisoner was taken to the Detective-office in charge of Detective Marsden, who has brought him over from America. After having some breakfast, which he partook of rather heartily, he was brought before Mr. T. S. Raffles, stipendiary magistrate, at the police court, Dale-street. The prisoner, who is a slightly-built man, with moustache and short black beard, was very pale and appeared very weak when placed in the dock.

Mr. Davies, deputy law-clerk to the watch committee, said that the prisoner was charged with having wilfully murdered his wife four years ago. He (Mr. Davies) did not propose to enter into the case, as the prisoner's attorney had applied for a remand for seven days.

Mr. Raffles.—Then there is no occasion to go into the case.

The prisoner was then removed from the dock.

It transpired that Mr. Cobb has been engaged as the prisoner's attorney.

After his hearing at the Liverpool Police Court on 7th September, Robert Reid was remanded in custody. His trial for murder was set to be heard at the Crown Court in St George's Hall, Liverpool in December of that year. Meanwhile, Detective Marsden resumed his usual duties in the Liverpool City Police. His return coincided with a gradual upsurge in Irish catholic nationalism headed by a group called the 'Fenian Brotherhood'. Known simply as 'Fenians', they were a precursor to the IRA and, it was rumoured, they had many sympathisers amongst the Irish immigrants living in Liverpool and the United States.

Animosity between Liverpool's Irish Catholic and Protestant population had rumbled on for decades. Fights and skirmishes between the two groups were a daily occurrence, whilst running street battles and riot during the St Patrick's Day and the Orange Day celebrations were an annual challenge for the police. Late in 1866 authorities in Liverpool began to be aware of rumours that weapons were being amassed by Fenians in Liverpool and police were placed on high alert. Archer (2011) tells us that in 1867 Liverpool's detectives were issued with revolvers, whilst muskets were sent to temporary police depots around the town. Detective Marsden became involved in the following cases in which Fenianism was suspected.

LIVERPOOL DAILY POST
5th October 1866

A FENIAN ASSAULT.—Charles Lee and Cecilia Lee, man and wife, were at the bar to answer a charge of dangerously assaulting Patrick Coffey and Thomas Maloney. — Detective Marsden deposed that on Wednesday night, having received information from the East Dispensary [hospital], he apprehended the prisoners in Rose-place, off Richmond-row, on a charge of assaulting two men with a poker.

—Mr. Walter: "Are the men able to appear?" —Marsden: "No, sir. One of them, Maloney, is lying in his own house in a dying state. The doctor says he was not likely to recover. Coffey is also very ill, but this morning is a little better".

—Ann Burns deposed that on Tuesday night, 12 o'clock, she was in Rose-place. She saw Lee and his wife rush out of the house and knock two men down with a poker. —Mr. Walter: "Did they both use the same poker?" Witness: "They each had poker, and they used them I can tell you".

—Mr. Walter: "What was the row about? Detective Marsden: "Fenianism was the cause of it. The two injured men and a lot of other people were singing Fenian songs, and they went to Lee's house and challenged him to come out and fight. They said if didn't they would 'burn the house down'. They said they had got a bottle of liquid which they would throw into the house and blow it up. They were saying all sorts of things like that, and as Lee did not came out, they ultimately burst his door open. Lee and his wife then rushed out with pokers, and began the attack."

—Mr. Walter asked that the prisoners might be remanded until the two men were able to appear. —Lee asked to be admitted to bail, but his worship replied that he could not grant the wish, as the men were in a very dangerous state. —The prisoners were accordingly remanded.

—In connection with this case a man named James Caine, was brought before the court at a later stage of the proceedings. Mr. Cobb appeared for this prisoner, and contended that the prisoner made no assault whatever upon either of the men, but that whilst he was at his supper heard a noise in the court where he lived, and on going out he saw a man assaulting his wife. —This prisoner was also remanded, and will be brought up with the Lees.

Lancashire Assizes Criminal Register, April 1866: Charles & Cecilia Lees and Maria & James Cain are jailed for 12 months for malicious wounding with a poker during a Fenian dispute.

Rose Place where Detective Marsden apprehended Charles and Cecilia Lee. They were bizarrely convicted for defending themselves from an attack by a Fenian catholic crowd threatening to burn their house down.

MINUTES OF THE HEAD CONSTABLE TO THE
LIVERPOOL WATCH COMMITTEE
5th December 1866

Transcription: *Detective Officers Jones and Marsden report for the information of the Divisional Superintendent Ride that they (Officers) have made inquiry respecting a letter addressed to him and signed Samuel Allport stating that a considerable quantity of muskets and bayonets were sent away on Saturday last from a house opposite to his in Birmingham. The officers found in the Goods Station of the London and North Western Railway Co., Park Lane, 50 cases containing Rifles which arrived at that station on Monday the 3rd instant., sent by Messrs Cooper and Goodman of Birmingham consigned to R Crooks & Co, 5 Molyneux Place, Liverpool. The cases are still in the Company's warehouse. Superintendent has promised to inform officers when they are removed and where to. Officers beg to add that R Crooks & Co. have for years received goods of this description to the knowledge of the railway officials. (© Liverpool Records Office, Liverpool Libraries.)*

Liverpool Assizes Court. Det. Marsden gave evidence in the Reid murder trial here in 1866. Picture courtesy of www.hiddenliverpool.co.uk

THE LANCASTER GAZETTE
22nd December 1866

THE LIVERPOOL WIFE MURDER. Robert Reid, 34, was indicted for having murdered his wife, in Liverpool, on the 4th of December, 1864. The prisoner was a tin-plate worker, and in December, 1862, he and his wife were living in a cellar in Lower Myrtle-street. They were on very bad terms, and according to the defence the wife was a woman of dissolute habits. Their children were in the workhouse; but on the occasion when the woman was killed the prisoner bad brought home one of them, a lad of 12 years old. On the part of the prosecution, a woman named Mary Rogers was called and stated that on the night of the 4th December 1864, she was in the prisoner's kitchen with the deceased, when the prisoner and the boy came in, about ten o'clock. The prisoner and his wife were sober. Witness [Rogers] had had some drink but knew all that passed. Prisoner said to witness, "Arrah, isn't this a fine lad?" Witness said he was. Prisoner sat down by the fire and asked the deceased to sing. She sang a song for him, and then be kissed the boy and hummed a song to himself. After this, he seized the deceased by the hair and pulled her towards the door. They did not speak to each other till the deceased said "Don't do that," and fell on her side near to the wall. Witness saw blood running from the deceased's arm and told the prisoner he had killed his wife. He did not answer but took the boy by the hand and said, "Johnny, come," and went away. She shouted "Murder" but never saw him again till he was in custody in New York. Deceased never spoke after she fell.

— A witness, named Mary Savage, who kept a shop near the prisoner's cellar, said she heard the singing, and afterwards a noise, as if a mug bad been broken against the wall. She went to the cellar and saw the deceased lying on the floor. — John Reid, the boy, stated

113

that the deceased, his mother, was abusive to his father on the night in question, and broke a jug over, his head. He left the cellar with the prisoner, and they slept at his uncle's, in Richmond Row, that night. Next day the prisoner was taken to the house of another uncle and was kept there till he was sent to New York. When deceased fell, she fell across a broken pan-mug, a jagged piece of which stood up like a spike. — A constable spoke of finding the deceased bleeding from a wound under the left arm, and to fetching a doctor. The broken mug was on the floor, but when witness saw it, it had its smooth side uppermost and was not near the deceased.

— Mary Adams, another neighbour, spoke to seeing the prisoner leaving his house on the occasion in question with a knife in his hand, and his hand covered with blood; and said she saw him put the knife down a sewer. — A detective officer proved that he found the knife in the sewer.

—Mr. Goodall Jones, surgeon, said he found two clean incised wounds in the deceased's arm, dividing the main artery; and the deceased died from loss of blood. Such wounds might have been inflicted with the knife produced, (or any other sharp instrument). The arm must have been raised when the stabs were given. It might have taken position either in striking or falling. The deceased was very lightly dressed. He did not think the broken mug could have caused the wounds.

— Detective Marsden, the officer who brought the prisoner from America, produced the following statement which the prisoner had made before a captain of police in New York:— "I Robert Reid, did not, in December, 1862, use any knife or weapon upon my wife or any other person. My wife was in a very bad state of health, drinking and stopping out at night. She was spitting blood four days previous to her death and threatened to throw herself and her child into the docks but was prevented by an officer. The child died three days afterwards. If I had injured her so as to have caused her death, I would not have gone and slept with her brother the same night, as I did. I have lost many a night's rest looking after her in the streets when she was out drunk."

— This was all the evidence in support of the charge. — The prisoner's counsel argued in support of the theory that the wounds had been caused by the deceased falling on the broken pan-mug; and contended that the Jury could not rely on the evidence of the woman Rogers, as they could on that of Savage and the boy. He held that there was no proof of malice; and that, even if the prisoner had stabbed the deceased, there was proof only of manslaughter. The learned Judge having summed up, the Jury asked the officer who was called to the cellar at the time, "In what state was Mary Rogers?" —The officer replied, "A little in liquor, but not drunk."— The Jury found the prisoner guilty, and the learned Judge passed the sentence of death.

Lancashire Assizes Criminal Register December 1866. Robert Reid is sentenced to: "death and his body to be buried within the precinct of the prison."

Kirkdale Gaol where Robert Reid was taken awaiting execution.

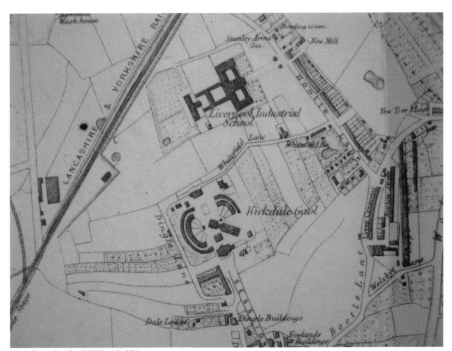

Kirkdale Gaol off Whitefield Lane.

CHAPTER 9

1867

1867 immediately begins with a shock development in the long-running Reid wife-murder case. Robert Reid who, on 12th January 1867 was due to be executed for his wife's killing, was suddenly granted a reprieve.

THE LEIGH CHRONICAL
1st January 1867

THE CONDEMNED CONVICT IN KIRKDALE GAOL.- There is one criminal in Kirkdale Gaol under sentence of death, passed upon him at the late Liverpool assizes. Robert Reid, the convicted wife murderer, will, unless a reprieve is received by the Sheriff in the meantime, be executed at Kirkdale on the 12th January. Since his condemnation he has been visited by his son, John Reid, a youth of 17 years of age, who gave evidence against him at the trial, by two cousins and a sister. It is stated that efforts are being made to obtain a reprieve for the unhappy man.

THE LONDON EVENING STANDARD
1st January 1867

THE CONDEMNED AT KIRKDALE.—The condemned criminal, Robert Reid, who was sentenced to death at the late assizes, for the murder of his wife in Lower Myrtle-street, four years ago, remains in the Kirkdale Gaol, and has been visited by his son, his sister from Ireland, and two cousins resident in Liverpool. He is attended by the Protestant chaplain, the Rev. R. Appleton. We understand that two petitions, praying for a commutation of the sentence, have been forwarded to the Home Office. One of the petitions was originated by the prisoner's friends, and is stated to have been numerously signed. However, so far, the authorities at the gaol have received no intimation which would lead them to believe that the extreme sentence of the law will not be carried into effect. The criminal still seems to entertain a hope that her Majesty's clemency will be extended towards him.—*Liverpool Albion.*

THE LIVERPOOL MERCURY
2nd January 1867

THE WIFE MURDER IN LIVERPOOL: REPRIEVE OF REID. We stated in Monday's impression that efforts were being made to obtain a commutation of the capital sentence passed upon Robert Reid at the last assizes, for the murder of his wife in a cellar in Lower Myrtle-street [formerly Thurlow Street] four years ago. The authorities seem to have considered this a fitting case for the exercise of her Majesty's clemency, a report having reached us last night to the effect that a reprieve for Reid had been received at the goal yesterday morning.

In the Reid case, the Home Office had received two appeals on behalf of Robert Reid pleading that the mandatory sentence of death in his case was harsh. It was argued that Eliza Reid had been a drunken, dissolute wife and mother, who had made at least one suicide attempt in the past. The authorities may have considered that Reid had acted under extreme provocation and had not intended to kill his wife when he struck her, but simply meant to teach her a lesson. Reid was therefore considered to be a candidate for the 'Royal Prerogative of Mercy' – more commonly known as 'Her Majesty's Clemency'. It is impossible to guess what Detective Marsden's feelings would have been about this turn of events. Considering the trouble and time he had taken in bringing back Reid from the United States, was he angry or exasperated about this outcome? Or was he sympathetic to Reid's situation?

LIVERPOOL DAILY POST
2nd February 1867

AN HOTEL THIEF.—John Graham, alias Henderson, a respectably dressed young man, who had the appearance of sailor, was brought up on remand, charged with having committed several hotel robberies in the town. On the 28th ult. the prisoner went to the Commercial Hotel, Union-street, and engaged lodgings there for the night, representing that on the following morning he was going to start for America in the ship Palmyra. The next morning Thomas Griffiths, a mariner, who had slept in room on same floor as the prisoner, missed 35s and an American cent, from his trousers pocket. He reported his loss to the landlady, and suspicion was attached to the prisoner; and a policeman was called in. The officer asked him what money he had, and he replied that when he went to bed, he had £7 8s. He produced his purse, and it was found to contain £8 4s. Upon being searched, the American cent which Griffiths had lost was found upon him, and he was therefore charged with stealing the whole of the money.

On the 23rd inst. the prisoner went to the Tiger Hotel, Dale-street, and engaged a bedroom for the night. He was shown to a bedroom which bad been occupied by the Rev. Malone, a catholic priest. The Rev. gentleman had been stopping at the hotel in December and left these on the 10th of the month for a journey to Manchester, leaving his travelling bag in the care of Mr. Fitzgerald, the landlord. He returned to Liverpool on Monday last, and on examining the bag found that the lock had been broken off, and silver "*pyx," two linen shirts, and a flannel shirt were missing. He reported his loss to the police on the following morning. Upon his describing the "pyx." the officers recollected that Mr. Benussi, Paradise-street, had sent in report that Friday, the 25th of January, that the prisoner had offered the "pyx" for sale at his shop. The "pyx" was therefore recovered, but the other articles were not. Police-constable 903 said he apprehended the prisoner on the 29th ult., and found in his possession a wedding-ring, **keeper, gold crucifix, and portion of a locket. The crucifix and the part of locket bad been left with the prisoner, who had since destroyed them. —Detective Jackson, reply to his worship, as to how it was that these things had been given to the prisoner after he was locked-up, explained that it often happened in cases where a crucifix was found upon prisoner, it was left with him, but not when the crucifix was valuable. — Detective Marsden said that that morning Miss Margaret Ellen Fitzgerald, and Miss Theresa Christina had, out of a number of persons, identified the prisoner as the person who slept in the room at the Tiger Hotel the 23rd January. These young ladies identified the keeper ring as having belonged to their deceased sister. The prisoner, who reserved his defence, was committed for trial at the sessions on the whole of these charges.

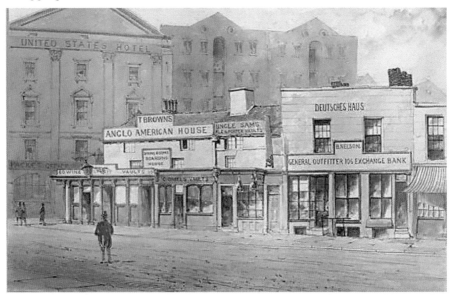

An example of the many hotels, boarding houses, outfitters and currency exchanges available to travellers in Liverpool during the 1860s. (Waterloo Road, WG Herdman)

*a 'pyx' is an ornamental container in which the Eucharist is kept.
**a 'keeper' is a close-fitting ring worn on the finger to prevent another - more valuable - ring from sliding off.

In the next news article in which Detective Marsden appears it can be seen that the Reid murder case continues to create work for him. In this instance, a girl called Mary Adams who had given evidence during the trial of Robert Reid on 22nd December 1866 (see previous chapter) had consequently become the target of revenge attacks by members of the local community.

THE DAILY POST
1st April 1867

ALLEGED PERSECUTION OF A WITNESS.—Mary Milend was charged with an assault on Mary Adams. Mr. Davies appeared for the prosecution, and Mr. Cobb for the defence. The prosecutrix, Mary Adams, had been the chief witness for the prosecution in the Thurlow-street murder case, tried-last Assizes, when a man named Reid was convicted of the murder of wife. She lives in Christian-street, and the prisoner in Lower Myrtle-street, late Thurlow-street, where the murder took place. The prosecutrix stated that a few days ago, about four o'clock in the afternoon, she was passing along in the neighbourhood when the prisoner, whom she did not know before, came up to her, called her "a transporting _____" , and said she would put her where Reid was. She then struck her on the head with a key and tore her dress, after which she ran off. In reply to the magistrate Elizabeth Kelly was examined for the defence, who stated that there was a row in which the prosecutrix and her sister were engaged with the prisoner and some others, and that the prosecutrix first caught the prisoner by the hair, and after a struggle the latter ran away. Witness and the prosecutrix had had a quarrel a few days before that also. The prosecutrix stated that whenever she and Elizabeth Kelly met, the latter called her "a transporting _____" and threatened to put her where Reid was. Detective Marsden stated that there was a strong animosity against the girl Adams among the people in that neighbourhood, on account of her having been a witness against Reid, and he had been obliged to go there several times on account of it. The case was remanded until this morning for further evidence to the assault.

THE LIVERPOOL DAILY POST
8th April 1867

TWO SOLDIERS CHARGED WITH HIGHWAY ROBBERY.— Charles Stewart and Thomas Parnell, two soldiers stationed at the North Fort, were brought up on remand, charged with an assault and robbery on Joseph Bremer, river pilot, resident in Cresswell-street, Everton. The assault took place on Monday night last, in Stanley-road, Kirkdale, and the prisoners were arrested next day and taken before Mr. Raffles, at the Police-court, when the main facts of the case were given in evidence and published. The evidence given on Saturday was of a corroborative character as to the identity of the prisoners. Several persons, who happened to be in Stanley-road, at the time the robbery was committed, gave evidence confirmatory of the identification of the prisoners. The landlord of a neighbouring public-house, in which the prisoners had been a short time previous to the robbery, identified them, and on the following morning a soldier's belt was found near the place, which belonged to Stewart. The prisoners were committed for trial at the assizes. Mr. Raffles observed that it ought to be known to the public, for it was highly creditable, that the non-commissioned officers and men of the detachment had expressed a wish to maintain the prosecutor during the time he would be prevented the injuries received from following his employment, and also to subscribe for providing him with a watch in place of that of which he had been robbed. Detective Marsden, who had charge of the case, stated that the pilot had declined the offer, at the same time expressing his thanks to the men.

An aerial view of the North Fort (Huskisson Dock). c1865

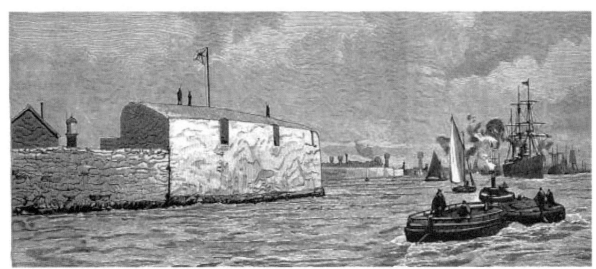

The North Fort built to defend Liverpool during the Napoleonic wars.

THE LIVERPOOL DAILY POST
20th July 1867

CHARGE OF ROBBING A SAILOR.—John Kelly, a man well known to the police, was charged with having robbed John Jones, a seaman, who lodges in Blundell-street. The prosecutor went into Mr. Tarbuck's public-house, in Warwick-street, on Thursday, and met several men, among whom was the prisoner. Prosecutor treated the men to some beer, and the prisoner subsequently offered to see him home. They left the house together, and while passing through Warwick-street, the prisoner forced the prosecutor against the wall, put his hand into his pocket, and abstracted a sovereign. Prisoner then ran away, and was apprehended the same evening by Detective-officer Marsden, and in reply to questions he said, "There are more Kellys than me. I am a sailor man myself and plough the salt sea for my living." The prosecutor, however, picked out the prisoner from a number of other men at the police-station. Prisoner was committed for trial.

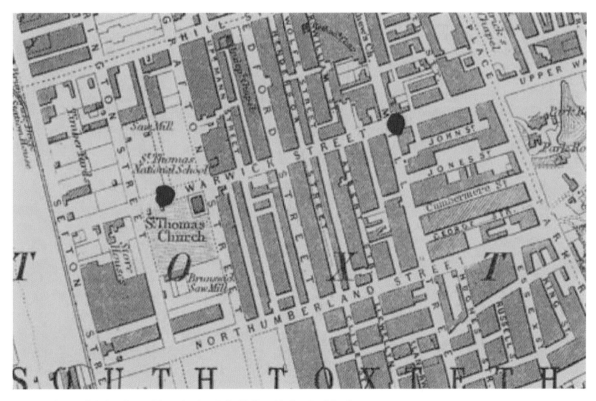

Warwick Street off Sefton Street, Toxteth where John Kelly robbed sailor John Jones.

THE LIVERPOOL DAILY POST
25th October 1867

The Ferocious Dog of Lower Bebington. Mr. John Henry Fuller, Heath Cottage, Lower Bebington again came before the court under summons charged with allowing a ferocious dog to be at large. The case was before the court on the previous Thursday, when it was deposed to that the dog had bitten eleven persons and alarmed seventeen. Mr. James, barrister, instructed by Mr. Seppings, on this occasion appeared for the defendant. The case had created great interest owing to the defendant having been some four or five times previously before the magistrates on similar charges. The dog was in court. It is a fine black animal, a beautiful specimen of the species. It wore a muzzle and kept a close proximity to Mr. and Mrs. Fuller.

The evidence taken on the inquiry the previous week was read over, in order to put Mr. James in possession of the full particulars of the case and afford to him opportunity of cross-examining the witnesses. Martha Norman's evidence stated that she was a single woman residing at New Ferry. On Tuesday, the instant, she was going along the highway, past Mr. Fuller's house, when the dog, now in court, came running out and pursued her, barking during the time. She ran to the policeman's gate, and he (the policeman) came to her assistance. The dog was not muzzled, and it frightened her very much .—Mr. James submitted the witness to a long cross-examination, the principal portion of which was as to whether she had any one with her on the night the dog made the attack upon her, which she stoutly maintained that no one "whatsomever" was with her. She did not know that she had seen the dog before, but she had heard of it biting people. It was public talk that it bit people.

— Police-officer 141 (Joseph Handford), in his evidence the previous week, had stated that Tuesday, the 8th instant, when at his own house, heard someone screaming in distress. On going out he found the last witness; the dog was in the middle of the road, barking, and that was the cause of the woman's fright. It had not a muzzle on. He had known the dog before. It had bitten eleven people before. He had had many neighbours complaining of the dog, and it had attacked other people. In the course of his cross-examination, the witness said it lived in the lodge belonging Mr. Clarke Aspinall. The first thing he saw when he left his own house was Martha Norman rushing through Mr. Aspinall's gate, and the dog was close behind her.

The defendant had been previously summoned about the dog. The levy was for £3 9s 6d, 40s the amount of costs and the rest for summonses. He had had several complaints by Mr. Clarke Aspinall about the dog. He had not asked Mr. Aspinall to attend the court, knowing that his business in Liverpool called him there, and (witness) had plenty of others to prove the ease. About the 16th June Mr. Aspinall told him that he dare not send his children past Mr. Fuller's house for fear of the dog, and that he had to send them another way. "Mr Fuller (to the defendant); "Is that the same dog you so faithfully promised to send away? On the 9th of May last you expressed yourself being very sorry to an annoyance to neighbours and said you would send the dog away."

— Mr. Barton "Before Mr. Coxon and myself, on the 9th of May, Mr. Fuller promised that the dog should be sent away. On the 6th of June, before Mr. Shaw and myself, the dog was here again: the same complaint was made, and the defendant was fined forty shillings and costs. and then promised that the dog should sent away. — Mr. Aspinall on the 20th September he promised faithfully that the dog should sent away, and that is the same dog.

William Scarisbrick, an old and infirm man, who it was said is still suffering from the injury and fright occasioned by an attack the dog had made upon him, stated that he was a retired farmer. The dog had bitten him early in the present year. That was "just the beginning of the dog;" he had not before that bitten many people. He was taking a walk out on the public road, and on passing Mr. Fuller's house, he saw the large black dog then in the court in the lane. It came from Mr. Fuller's premises. The dog seized him by the arm and bit him, leaving a black mark. He (witness) was tremendously frightened. —In cross-examination the witness said the dog laid hold of his arm and had not been for friends he would have worried him. He (witness) would go miles round rather than pass Mr. Fuller's house again. The reason he had not taken a summons out against Mr. Fuller was that he did not like to appear before the magistrates, for he had been very poorly ever since was bitten.

— James Oake, a plumber, living New Ferry, stated that he found the dog worrying [attacking] the old gentleman (the previous witness). The dog had got him against a wall. He was going throw stones at the dog when a little girl from Mr. Fuller's house went between the dog and the old man. The dog went away with the girl. The dog was not muzzled. Mrs Fuller was there, and he (witness) remonstrated with her, telling her that she ought to ashamed of herself to keep a dog like that, and told her that if Mr. Scarisbrick did not take steps against it, he (witness) would. "Mr. James: You speak of the dog worrying the old man, where had he got hold of him?—Witness: He got hold of him by the arm, the same if was worrying cat. I do not know whether you ever saw cat worried?"—Mr. James: "yes I have; many."

— Edward Jones, of Higher Bebington, deposed to having been attacked by the dog twelve months previously, when the beat it off with an umbrella. Mrs. Fuller and a girl came out the house, and he told the former what had occurred, and she seemed quite saucy

.— Mr. Joseph who described himself as accountant residing at Bebington, offered himself in evidence. He said, "I have come forward to say that the inhabitants of Bebington are in a state of alarm with respect to the dog. I have not come to speak of any individual case, but the general character of the dog. I know the dog; it is the one I see here to-day. I am afraid of passing the house for fear of the dog, and my family also are much alarmed. The dog has never attacked me."

Samuel Oake, a joiner, who in May last was working at Mr. Fuller's house, deposed to the dog having made an attack upon him, seized him by the arm, bit him, and caused him to bleed, and he was unable to attend to business for eleven days. He saw Mr. Fuller about it and took him a note for his loss of time, but he would not pay it.

Mr. John Jenkins, who stated that he was a merchant, also spoke of the vicious character of the dog. Other evidence of a like nature was tendered. The Chairman said that the bench had come to the determination to order an indictment to taken out and to send the case to the Quarter Sessions at Knutsford in January next. Mr. James said that the information was one based upon an Act of Parliament which provided a certain penalty or punishment, and they must either dismiss the summons or convict.

The Chairman: "We order the summons to stand over.—Mr. James: "Do I understand you that you will not allow the defendant to go into his case now?"—The Chairman: "No, certainly not".

—Mr. James then said that Mr. Fuller wished to be set right as to the alleged arrangements which had been made relative to the dog. It was perfectly true that some time ago Mr. Fuller had, at the request of their worships, undertaken to part with the dog. His partner, Mr. Kemp, was present in court, and when they got out [of the court] Mr. Fuller, in the presence of his attorney, gave the dog away to Mr. Kemp. Mr. Kemp happened at the time to staying with Mr. Fuller, and therefore the dog remained for a time at Mr. Fuller's house.

For some reason or other Mr. Fuller seemed to be the subject of much spite on the part of the inhabitants of Bebington, for on the night of the day on which the dog was given away, he was returning to his own house, when he was knocked down, brutally ill-treated, and left in state of insensibility. Mr. Fuller very properly put the matter into the hands two of the most able and intelligent detective officers in Liverpool (Marsden and Fitzsimmons), and they told him by no means to part with the dog—that if he parted with it; such was the state of the neighbourhood, that his house would not safe. It was for that reason, and that reason alone, that Mr. Fuller had kept the dog.

—The Chairman said Mr. Fuller had been there [at the court] three times since May, and had had plenty of opportunity for stating that before. After a long conversation relative to certain costs made for the fine imposed by Mr. Fuller, the case was closed. After it had done so, Marsden, the detective officer from Liverpool, wished make a statement. He said he had been summoned to the court by Mr. Fuller to give evidence. He said about three weeks ago Mr. Fuller's partner, Mr. Kemp, came to him in Liverpool. Marsden was about to get on omnibus when Mr. Kemp came up and asked him if he had heard about Mr. Fuller, and then told him that gentleman had been dangerously assaulted. Marsden replied, "If Mr. Fuller's life is in danger, if I were you I would not part with the dog."—The Chairman asked: "You did not advise him, knowing that the magistrates had ordered the dog to be destroyed, to keep it?" — Marsden: "Certainly not. I was here in September, and Mr. Fuller said he would part with the dog." —The Chairman: "That only makes the case worse".

Heath Cottage. Home of the ferocious dog of Lower Bebington.

CHAPTER 10

1868

THE CARMARTHEN WEEKLY REPORTER
7th March 1868

A YOUNG GENTLEMAN KILLED BY AN AMERICAN CAPTAIN. The police were engaged up to a late hour on Friday night in investigating the circumstances attending the death of a young gentleman who was well known in Liverpool and Southport, and who is said to have been killed by a blow which he received from an American captain in a row which took place in a public-house in Liverpool. The affray took place on Monday night, and the gentleman died on the following day: but the authorities seem to have known nothing of the matter until Thursday, when their attention was directed to it by some gentlemen who live in Southport and who knew the deceased, who resided at that place. It is also somewhat strange that no inquest has been held, especially if it were known that the young man's death was the result of a violent treatment. The facts of the melancholy affair seem to be as follows— A young gentleman named Mr. T. Carstairs, who resided with his friends at Southport, was in Liverpool on Monday night, with a friend, with whom he went to the theatre. After leaving the theatre, he and his friend went to the Theatre Tavern, in Williamson-square. While sitting in the snug, it is said that Mr. Carstairs commenced singing "The Bonnie Blue Flag" - a song which was exceedingly popular with the friends of the South during the late American war. A number of American captains were in the house at the time, and they seem to have become offended with Mr. Carstairs for singing a "Secession song." - They told him to desist, but it is alleged that he declined to do so, and that being requested, he proceeded to sing the song a second time. A row then took place, glasses were thrown about, and some severe injuries were inflicted by the combatants upon each other. One of the persons in the melee was knocked through a glass door, and in the thick of the fight it is said that an American captain seized a champagne bottle and gave Mr. Carstairs a violent blow on the head with it. Ultimately the disturbance was quelled, and Mr. Carstairs was removed as soon as possible to Southport, where he died on Tuesday from the effects, it is supposed, of the blow he received from the American. Detective Inspector Carlisle and Detectives Melling and Marsden are, by the instructions of Mr. Kehoe, making inquiries into the matter, and it is to be hoped that they will succeed in apprehending the man who struck the fatal blow, although it is said that one of the Americans engaged in the affair has sailed in his vessel for the United States.

American sailors. During the nineteenth century they disembarked at Liverpool each day in their thousands.

ANNUAL LICENCING SESSION. The annual session for the granting of publicans' licences in the borough of Liverpool was held at the Police Courts, Dale Street. Mr. J. B. Brancker occupied the chair, and the following other magistrates were present :—Messrs. J. H. Turner, N. Caine, T. Dover, E. Lawrence. A Castellain, E Samuelson, J. Woodruff, R Sheil, Joseph Cooper, George Melly, A Turner, H. Tunnicliffe, W. Crosfield, Lamport, J.G Livingston, and J. R. Jeffery. The Court proceeded to hear the applications made from persons residing in the following wards Rodney-street, Abercromby, Lime-street, St Anne-street, West Derby, Toxteth, and North Toxteth.

THE DEATH OF MR. CARSTAIRS. Elizabeth Quigley, of No. 12, Williamson-square, applied for a renewal her spirit license. —Mr. Pemberton appeared in support of the application. —Detective Inspector Carlisle stated that in consequence of a statement made to him by the applicant's barmaid, he discovered that on the night of Monday, 17th February last, a song was being sung in room in the applicant's public-house in which were a number of American captains. A disturbance took place between the captains and a young gentleman named Carstairs and he (Carstairs) was struck the head with a bottle. He died a day or two afterwards at Southport and no inquest was held. He (Inspector Carlisle) traced the throwing of the bottle to a captain who could have been apprehended had an inquest been held. He (Inspector Carlisle) had visited the house on some occasions and found women of ill-repute drinking at the bar. The house was next door to the Theatre Royal and he wished to remind the bench that when the disturbance to which he referred occurred, if Mrs. Quigley or her assistants had called in the police, in all probability Mr. Carstairs would not have been assaulted. There were three or four policemen on duty near the theatre and one of them was quite near at the time.

—In reply to Mr. Pemberton, Inspector Carlisle said that he knew that Mr Carstairs went to his mother's house in Southport and died there. He had also heard it reported that the young gentleman had died of natural causes. -Mr. Caine: "What is the character generally of the house? Is it visited by prostitutes?" —Inspector Carlisle: "Whenever I visited it I found it so." —The Inspector further stated, in reply to Mr. Pemberton, that he was not aware that any information (complaint) had been laid against the house during the last twelve months.—Mr. Jeffrey, referring to the question put by Mr. Caine, said that surely that gentleman would not say that public-house doors must be shut against women of certain class who asked to be supplied with drink. If there were any violation of the law—if the women misconducted themselves in the house—there was remedy.—Inspector Carlisle, in answer to the question, said that the women whom he saw at the applicant's house were standing there very quietly drinking what they had ordered, and were conducting themselves very well.—Mr. Pemberton: "Though they saw you there? They recognise you, some of them, I daresay?"—Inspector Carlisle: Very often, sir. —Mr. Pemberton said be wished to impress upon the bench the fact that the women did not assemble for any improper purpose; and added that he doubted if there had been an infraction of the law.
(To Inspector Carlisle): "Have you ever seen respectable persons there?" —Insp Carlisle: "Yes; I have seen number of young gentlemen

there."—Mr. Pemberton again reminded the bench that no information (complaint) had been laid against the house within the last 12 months.

Williamson Square. The building on the left is the Theatre Tavern where Thomas Carstairs was fatally injured in a fight with American sailors.

—Mr. Wybergh said the real charge against the applicant was that in her house a gentleman was assaulted and it was supposed his death resulted as a consequence of that assault. There was a police report on the subject and it would set forth all the circumstances attending the case. He (Mr. Wybergh) thought the bench ought to hear the whole of the circumstances.—Mr. Pemberton objected to the report as not being legal evidence.—Mr. Wybergh said there was very important question involved in the case. It seemed to him that neither Mr. Pemberton nor any other advocate ought to interpose between the bench and the police officers who gave information as to the respectability and conduct of persons asking for licenses. Magistrates were required by Act of Parliament to grant licenses to fit persons and they very properly required their officers to furnish them with reports. There was another reason as too why the report should be read. Supposing the decision of the bench were appealed against; the case on the part the magistrates would be that the license was refused because of the facts contained in a certain police report. It was therefore necessary that the report should be read out in order that the magistrates might know what it was about.

—Mr Pemberton: Your worships will take note that I object to having it read.

—The reports, which were as followed, were then read:

"EXTRACT FROM POLICE SOUTH TOWN DIVISION REPORT BOOK, MARCH 17, 1868.

Detective-inspector Carlisle and Detective-constable Marsden beg respectfully to report for the information of Mr. Superintendent Kehoe, that from instructions received from him to make a strict inquiry respecting the assault which was supposed to have led to the death of Thomas Philip Carstairs, took place in Quigley's public-house, 12 Williamson-square, about midnight on Monday, 17th February, through some missile having been thrown at him by a man unknown. They (the officers) have made a most careful investigation of the facts connected with the assault and beg to submit the following as the substance of their inquiry:

"Mr. Thomas P. Carstairs resided with his mother at Southport and spent the evening of the 17th February at the Alexandra Theatre in this town. When the performance was over, he proceeded to the Tithebarn-street Station to return to Southport, but he discovered the train had left. He then returned and engaged lodgings for the night at the Stork Hotel, Queens-square. At about twelve o'clock he left the hotel and sauntered into Williamson-square and entered the public-house kept by Elizabeth Quigley. In a back parlour were a number of men, among whom were several American sea captains. A difference arose from a song being sung called "The Bonny Blue Flag". Some chaffing followed and it ended in a kind of general row; blows were struck, a glass door, a champagne bottle used for holding water and some tumbler glasses

127

were broken. Mr. Carstairs, in the *melee* received a blow on the nose, it is supposed from a tumbler glass thrown at him by some of the captains. This disturbance lasted only a few minutes and no information could be satisfactorily obtained as to who threw the glass. A few minutes after, Mr. Carstairs left the house and was met by a policeman, who took him in a car (carriage) to the Infirmary, his wounds were dressed, and he returned to the Stork Hotel. He obstinately refused to give any information to the police beyond that he had received the cut in a general row. This public-house is nightly frequented by flash prostitutes who are served at the bar or counter, but are not permitted to enter any other room in the house. Had the barman or barwoman (the only persons in charge at the time) called in the police, the disturbance would have been quelled and probably the assault upon Mr. Carstairs would have been prevented. Mr. Jeffery asked that if the row only occupied a few minutes and the young man left immediately after, where was the reflection (blame) upon the keeper of the public-house for not calling in the police? The young man had gone.

—Mr. Wybergh said there another report which was as follows:—
"EXTRACT POLICE SOUTH TOWN DIVISION BOOK FEBRUARY 29, 1868. "Inspector Hough reports that constable No.689 states that at about 12 o'clock am on the 18th instant, he saw Mr. Carstairs run out of Quigley's public-house with his hand to his head and was bleeding very much. Police-constable asked him what was the matter. He answered, 'I have got a cut the on the head with a glass.' The police-constable asked him if he knew who had done it. He said, 'No.' He at first declined to go the Infirmary, but afterwards consented, and was taken there. The Inspector came up shortly after the occurrence and visited the house to ascertain the facts of the case. He was informed by the barman that he saw a man throw the glass but did not know his name or address and could give the Inspector no further information."

Mr. Jeffery said he did not think the keeper of the public-house could have prevented the row. If there was any reflection (blame) it was on the police for not entering the house at once. There were no women in the room in which the occurrence took place. —Mr. Caine asked if there could be propriety of conduct where improper women were assembled? —Mr. Jeffery: "The women must exist and we must give them shelter. If we thrust them into the streets we should make them ten times worse than they are now."—The question was then put to the vote.
—For the granting of the license, Messrs. Jeffery, Lawrence, Woodruff, and Tunnicliffe—4. Against, Messrs. Brancker, Caine, Castellain, Bennett, J. H. Turner, and A Tamer—6. The renewal consequently refused.

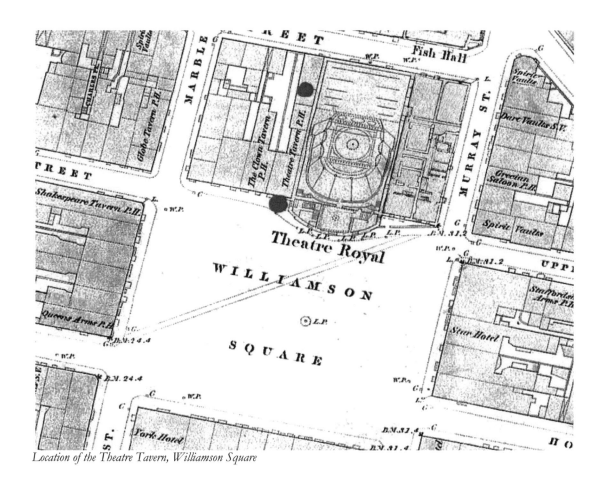

Location of the Theatre Tavern, Williamson Square

Williamson Square and the Theatre Royal by WG Herdman

129

EXTENSIVE PLUNDER BY PAWN-BROKERS ASSISTANT.

—A respectable looking young man, named Joseph Cronstan, was brought up. He appeared overwhelmed with shame, and immediately on being put to the bar, leaned his head on the iron rail in front of it and became much agitated. Scarcely had he made his appearance than a well-dressed and lady-like looking young woman, who sat with a female friend on the form at the side of the court to the right of the magistrate's seat, at the back the reporters' box, shrieked out, and fell from the seat to the floor of the court. In a short time she became pacified, and the charge was proceeded with.

—Mr. Walter, the prosecuting solicitor, said the prisoner was assistant to Mr. John Beeseley, pawnbroker in Fox-street, and he had been in that employ for the last 13 months. It appeared that during that time he had been robbing his employer to a large extent, and, as it appeared by his own account, in the following way. When a customer went to redeem goods, he presented a ticket, of which there is counterfoil placed on the goods pledged. The prisoner the took the money lent the goods with the interest and destroyed the tickets. The other day Mr. Beeseley saw the prisoner buy a valuable gold watch over the counter, and his suspicions, in consequence, were aroused. He consulted with Marsden (detective officer), who went to the house of the prisoner's mother. Whilst there the prisoner came in, and said, "Come, Marsden, I have seen Mr. Beeseley," and they went together to Mr. Beeseley's shop, where the prisoner was charged with having stolen £50 belonging to his employer. He said he had done so and had given the money to a young lady £10 at a time.

Marsden went to Crewe, he saw the young girl who had just cried out in court. She came over with the officer to Liverpool, and produced a valuable gold chain, some jewellery, ornaments, and a considerable sum of money, which she said she had received from the prisoner. He (Mr. Walter) did not purpose that day to call the young lady, but to ask his worship, after he had heard the evidence of Marsden, for a remand.

—Detective Marsden stated that on Saturday Mr. Beeseley spoke to him with respect to the prisoner robbing him. They proceeded the house of the prisoner's mother, in Warwick-street. The prisoner came in, and seeing him, whom he had known for a length of time, he said, "Marsden, I have seen Mr. Beeseley; let's go to the shop." He (Marsden) told him was charged with stealing £50 belonging to Mr. Beeseley. "Well," he said, "I have taken the money and destroyed the tickets. I gave the money to a young lady, Miss Brett, of Crewe." He (Marsden) went to Crewe the previous night and came with her by the nine o'clock train to Liverpool. They proceeded to the house of her uncle, where she produced in gold, and jewellery to the value of about £30.

—The prisoner was remanded for seven days.

ROBBERY BY A BARMAN.—"Only Breach of Trust."— Edwin Taylor, a young man said to be respectably connected, his friends residing in Manchester, was brought up on the charge of stealing a cash-box containing £53 10s, belonging to Mr. Peter Leech, licensed victualler, Lodge-lane, Edge-hill. Mr. Davies, deputy law-clerk to the Watch Committee, conducted the prosecution. In opening the case, he remarked that the prisoner was a barman at the house of the prosecutor, where he was engaged on Thursday last, having been highly recommended. Between three and four o'clock on Wednesday afternoon Mrs. Leech asked her husband for some money to go shopping and having supplied her from a safe in the bar, he went upstairs to the sitting-room, forgetting that he had left his keys in the door of the safe. The prisoner was in the bar at this time. About twenty minutes after Mr. Leech had been in the sitting-room, a little girl went up him, and in consequence of something she told him, he went down and found that the barman was not at the counter. On examining the safe discovered that a cash-box, which contained £25 in silver, and £23 10s in gold, was missing.

The prisoner had absconded from the place and the prosecutor gave immediate information to the police, and the same evening Taylor was apprehended by Detective Marsden. Mr. Davies added that the prisoner had purchased a quantity wearing apparel from the shop of Messrs. Lewis and Co., outfitters, where he left the cash-box. On being charged with the robbery, he replied, " Oh, its only a breach of trust" — Mr. Leech stated that on Thursday last he engaged the prisoner as his barman, having received a recommendation for him from Mr. Rylance, late a detective officer in Liverpool. On Wednesday afternoon the witness had given his wife some money to go shopping, and went upstairs, leaving the prisoner in the bar. He also left his keys in the safe there, forgetting that he had done so. After he had been in the sitting-room a short time he heard knocking downstairs but thought it was the children at play. At length his little girl came up and told him he was wanted downstairs. Going down, he found a coachman at the door, who told him there was no one in the bar. Witness then went into the cellar and other parts the premises, searching for Taylor, but he was not to be found. Examining the safe, he missed the cash-box, which contained £25 in silver and 10s in gold. He then gave information of the robbery to a policeman, at the same time getting friend keep watch for the prisoner at Lime-street station. —A cash-box and purse were here produced, and identified by Mr. Leech. The magistrate, addressing the prisoner: "Do you wish me to try you now, or will you for trial the sessions?"— Taylor: "I would sooner have it done with now". —An assistant in the shop of Messrs. Lewis and Co. said the prisoner went there about four o'clock on Wednesday afternoon and purchased clothing to the amount of about £4 and had no coat and hat on when he went there. He came in a cab and had a cash-box with him. As he left the latter [cash-box] on the counter, the witness asked him about it, when he said he wished leave there. Witness then inquired what its contents were and was told that it was empty. Detective Marsden stated, that having received information of the robbery, he went to Edge Hill, and then Walton. Returning in consequence of some information received, he proceeded to Wavertree, with the intention of seeing a friend of the prisoner. At the door of person's house he found a cab, inquiring the driver what he was doing there, he was told that he was waiting for two gentlemen from Manchester. Entering the house, Marsden found the prisoner sitting on the sofa drunk and when Marsden charged him with the robbery, replied, "Oh, it's only breach of trust." £39 10d were found in his possession. —He now pleaded guilty and was sentenced six months' imprisonment.

Wavertree High Street with its Georgian shopfronts, early twentieth century.

Wavertree was a village on the outskirts of Liverpool in 1868. Detective Marsden apprehended Edwin Taylor here after a lengthy chase around Liverpool from Edge Hill to Walton and then to Wavertree.

THE MANCHESTER COURIER AND THE
LANCASHIRE CENTRAL ADVERTISER
17th September 1868

ELOPEMENT IN HUMBLE LIFE. CAPTURE OF THE RUNAWAYS. An elopement of a not very romantic character took place on Saturday from the colliery district near Durham. It seems that at Dix Pit Colliery, near Fence-houses, in the parish of Lumley, there have resided for many years past two families, named Temple and Stokes. The heads of these families were on very friendly neighbourly terms and went in and out of one another's houses in the usual free and unsophisticated manner that exists in country villages. Then, again, the children of the two families were often playing together, and altogether presented appearance of felicity that poets love to dwell upon. Mr. Andrew Temple is a pitman, and a very hardworking man and William Stokes was his companion at the same pit. Temple had been married his wife for 27 years, and had had 14 children, one of whom was married; and Stokes was married, but had not such a large family, his children numbering only six.

On Saturday last Temple went to work as usual in the pit, and, on his return in the evening, missed his wife, a "very clever, careful woman," according to his account, from her usual place by the fireside. As she did not return in reasonable time, he made some inquiries, and then found out that Mr. Stokes, who had not been at work that day, was also "from home." His suspicions that all was not as it should be were now excited for the first time, and he returned home to make an examination and see if had lost anything more besides his wife. He looked about him, and then missed his hard-earned savings, amounting about £100, a gold watch, a silver watch, two gold chains, and all his wife's wearing apparel. Next morning he proceeded with one of his sons to Newcastle in search the runaways, but notwithstanding that used all diligence he was not able to find them then secured the services of Sergeant Thompson, of the Durham county constabulary, and carried on to Liverpool, the place to which so many erring people make their way, leaving his son as the look-out at Newcastle.

On the arrival of Temple and Thompson here they communicated with the police, and Detective-officer Robert Marsden was appointed to assist them in their search. They proceeded at once to the docks, and seeing a steamer starting off for America, got into a small boat and boarded her, but without any successful result, as the parties wanted were not among the passengers. Disappointed, the parties returned to the shore, and walked about the town in all the neighbourhoods likely to approve attractive to strangers, but again without avail. Yesterday the search continued, and the 'City of Antwerp' (an Inman steamer for New York) was examined. Here the errand of the parties was announced, and the passengers aided in the hunt for the runaways.

All at once Temple spied out his faithless wife and her paramour, and going up to Stokes shook hands with him, immediately after which he said "I mun' have thee transported for this," and then turning to his wife he told her he should turn her adrift. Mrs. Temple did not seem to care about this, for she commenced calling her husband a "blackguard" and Stokes a "gentleman". The passengers aboard the steamer were all this time laughing and jeering at the parties, and suggesting different modes of dealing with them, especially when it was known what large families the runaways had left behind. Surprise was also expressed that Stokes, who is a tall, fine-looking man of 38 years of age, should have run away with Mrs. Temple, who a very ordinary-looking woman, and 47 years of age.

The party were all landed, when they proceeded to the Detective-office, Dale-street.

Here Stokes and Mrs. Temple were examined, and upon them found money, a passage ticket for New York the names of Matthews, 38 years age, and Sarah Matthews, 35 years age, and a bill for board and lodgings at the house of Mr. J. Bowles, Lord Nelson-street, where they had been staying together as husband and wife from the 12th to the 16th Sept. In the box of luggage that was recovered was found, in addition Mrs. Temple's clothing, a suit of new clothes for Stokes and gun belonging to Stokes, who was found to be wearing a gold watch and chain belonging to Temple. When charged with stealing the money and watch, Stokes said he did not steal the money, and the watch was given to him by Mrs. Temple. Mr. Stokes and Mrs. Temple were then locked in the main Bridewell and will be removed to their own county in the course of to-day. It was stated that this was the third time eloping couples had been stopped on board the *City of Antwerp*, either by the police or their relatives.

The transatlantic steamer 'City of Antwerp'.

Princes Dock and its floating Landing Stage from where Stokes and Temple (and many other couples) attempted to elope to the United States.

DISGRACEFUL CONDUCT.—An elderly man named Alexander Black, was placed in the dock, charged with feloniously receiving a quantity of wearing apparel and bed-clothing belonging to the Select Vestry of Liverpool, and was further charged with stealing blankets, towels, and a very large quantity of other property belonging to Messrs. D. and C. MacIver and Co., the well-known shipowners. Mr. Walter conducted the prosecution, and it would seem from his statement that the prisoner had been guilty of very base, ungrateful conduct, as far as Messrs. MacIver were concerned. It appears that he was for a long time employed as baker on board the Cunard ships sailing from this port, and as got into years, Messrs. MacIver pensioned him off, as it may be termed—allowed him to retire from that calling, paid him £1 per week, and let him do any little odd job he liked on board the steamers when they were in port. Some days ago, Detectives Marsden and Fox received information that some wearing apparel had been stolen from the Brownlow-hill Workhouse, and that there was reason to suppose some part of it would be found in the possession the prisoner.

On Thursday they searched his house in Opie-street, Everton, and there, sure enough, the stolen articles were found. The officers also discovered there blankets, towels, rice, sugar, indeed a cart load of goods, which had been stolen from time to time from the ships and premises of the prosecutors. Marsden then went down to the Dock and apprehended the old rascal, finding upon him several wax candles he had purloined from one of Messrs. MacIver's vessels. On being charged with stealing the property alluded to, he said, "Well, Marsden, whatever you found of course I brought away." - These facts having been proved in evidence, the magistrate, addressing the prisoner, said, "You've made a very ungrateful return for the kindness shown to you."

Marsden: "He told me he did it through poverty; but when we searched the house we found plenty of beef, bread, and other things there, which showed he was not very poor".— Black was remanded for seven days, that the police have time to make further inquiries. He had nothing whatever to say in his defence.

Liverpool Workhouse, Brownlow Hill c1930. This site is now occupied by the Liverpool Metropolitan Cathedral.

CHAPTER 11

1869

Omnibus, The Strand. Cattle unloaded from ships being driven to market. Late nineteenth century. © Liverpool Records Office, Liverpool Libraries.

THE LIVERPOOL DAILY POST
13th February 1869

CHARGE OF EMBEZZLEMENT AGAINST A BOY. William Arthur Griffiths, a good-looking, respectably dressed lad about 15 or 16 years of age, whose friends reside in Rishton street, Breckfield-road, was brought the charge of having embezzled several sums of money belonging to Messrs. Shaw, Bishop, and Co., ship and insurance brokers, 22, Fenwick-street. The case was not gone into, remand being applied for. It was ascertained that the prisoner had been in the prosecutors'

office as apprentice or junior clerk during the past two years. Latterly suspicions were entertained as to his honesty, it being thought that he had been guilty of misappropriating money belonging to them, though the matter had been overlooked out of consideration for his parents, who are highly respectable people. He was missed from the office in January, and on the 20th of that month the prosecutors received the following letter:

"Messrs. Shaw, Bishop, and Co. Sikh,—By the time you receive this I shall be in a ship on its way to Melbourne, having made the sea my home. I had the *Mexican's* [a ship] and another small entry [payment], altogether amounting to about £4. and some odd pence, to make late on Saturday, so I left it till Monday, when I found I'd lost the money. Not caring to tell you, and I knew my mother was too poor to repay that amount, waited until I received some more money for entries and got money from the *France [a ship]*. The *Mexican* having sailed. I took the *France's* money (£1) and some other entries and passed the *Mexican*, and since then I have committed theft, you will see by the Customs receipt. Praying that you will keep this from my mother, who is in a decline, and forgive me, and my wages due £2 10s, will cover some. —I remain, in haste, W. A. Griffiths.

Messrs. Shaw and Co. caused inquiries to be made, and discovered that the lad had embezzled about £8, given to him for the purpose of paying dues in respect of the entry of various goods. The police were then communicated with, and they were not long in learning that Griffiths had not gone to sea but was in London. He returned to Liverpool a day or two since, and that (Friday) morning was apprehended by Detective Marsden. He now declined to make any reply to the charge preferred against him and was remanded for seven days.

It is possible to deduce from this garbled letter that clerk William Griffiths had received a £4 payment from a ship called the *Mexican* which he was meant to enter into his company's ledger. He didn't do this and then lost the money. He then used the money from another ship called the *France* to pay the money he had lost. He then decided to flee and left a false trail by claiming he had gone to Australia. What is notable about this case is that it again highlights the disparity between the type of language used by Victorian journalists when reporting cases regarding those who were 'respectable' and those who were not. For example, it is William Griffiths' personal appearance, ie, being 'good-looking and respectably dressed' which sets the tone for the report which follows. Although he had been suspected of stealing from his employers for some time, no action had been taken due to his parents being highly respectable people. This contrasts with descriptions found in the *Liverpool Daily Post* and *Liverpool Mercury* in that same year which describe "a wretched-looking woman charged with assault"; "an elderly woman, of repulsive appearance charged with keeping a brothel", and "a brutal-looking fellow charged with stealing 1s 6d from a boy." Again, this reinforces the idea that appearance and respectability were one and the same thing. Collectively, this type of reporting emphasised the idea that criminality and respectability were mutually exclusive.

THE LIVERPOOL DAILY POST
17th March 1869

THE THROWING OF PARAFFIN OIL BY A WIFE ON HER HUSBAND. DEPOSITION OF THE INJURED MAN. As we stated yesterday, the man named Michael Crowley, who was severely burned on Saturday evening by his wife, Mary Ann Crowley, by throwing a bottle of paraffin oil over him, was found to have been severely scorched and that he is not expected to recover. Yesterday morning Mr. T. Raffles, stipendiary magistrate, attended the Royal Infirmary, along with Mr. Roberts, magistrates' clerk, for the purpose of taking Crowley's deposition.

Michael Crowley, on being sworn, deposed:— "I have been living in No. 1, Lonsdale-street. The prisoner is my wife. On the night of the 13th instant I came home a little intoxicated. I wanted to go out and asked my wife to go and bring some things we had in pledge. She refused to go so and hit her with my fist on the head with the left hand. She turned round; there was a bottle of paraffin oil on the table, and she threw it right at me unawares. I mean my back was towards her, and I did not know she was going to do it, or I should have stopped her. I found myself all in blaze. I ran out into the street. I did not become insensible. In reply to the deposition of the prisoner (Mary Ann Crowley) he stated: —"I only hit you once. I did not beat you on the sofa and throw you down. It was you that threw the plate at me". The prisoner, who has been remanded, will be brought up again before the magistrates to-morrow.

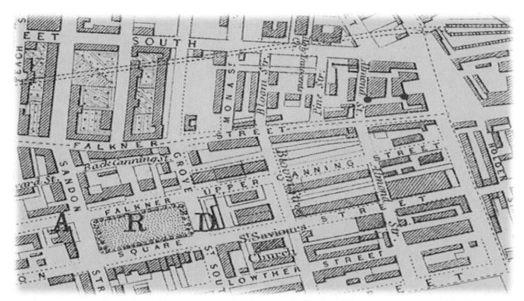

Lonsdale Street off Almond Street, Toxteth. Scene of the 'man on fire' killing. This site is now occupied by the Liverpool Women's Hospital.

Liverpool Infirmary, Brownlow Street. Michael Crowley taken here with severe burns after he was set alight with paraffin oil thrown by his wife. This site is now occupied by the Waterhouse Building of the University of Liverpool.

138

THE FATAL CASE OF BURNING BY PARAFFIN OIL. COMMITTAL OF DECEASED'S WIDOW FOR MANSLAUGHTER.

Yesterday (Tuesday) morning, Mary Anne Crawley was brought up before Mr. Raffles, the stipendiary magistrate, at the Dale-street police court charged with the manslaughter of her late husband, Michael Crawley, a jobbing builder, living at No. 1, Lonsdale-street. Mr. Davies prosecuted. The prisoner, who seemed to be fully aware of her position, appeared to be in delicate health, and was accommodated with a chair in the dock.

The following evidence was heard:- Matthew Woodcock said-I live at 28, Almond-street. I am assistant to my father, who keeps a coal yard. On Saturday night, the 13th instant, about a quarter past ten, I was in the coal yard, which is about five doors from deceased's house. Prisoner came into the coal yard at that time. I asked her what she wanted - coming into my father's coal yard to make rows [a fight]. She was sober. She rushed into me in a fright, and I thought her husband was following her. I went to the door of the coal yard, and saw deceased coming out of his own house on fire. He went past me. He was running roaring out for help. He ran along Lonsdale Street to Crown Street I went after him and I did not get up to him until he fell down on his knees at Crown-street, he was blazing all through. I saw some man go up to him, and when I got to him the flames were quenched. When I saw he was attended to I went back. I asked the prisoner what way the fire took place. That was before I ran after him - when I went to the door and saw him coming out of his house in a blaze. I asked her how did he come to be on fire. She said, "I think some of the oil got into the fire and took to him."' She did not say anything further.

Elizabeth Hughes said - I am the wife of William Hughes, butcher, 22 Almond-street. One of my windows looks into Lonsdale-street, I can see deceased's house from my window. I remember the night of Saturday, the 13th instant. About a quarter-past ten I saw deceased running past my window all on fire. I did not know who it was at the time. I ran out and after him. I turned back. There was a crowd at our door and I asked who was the man. The prisoner said, "It's Crawley, of course." I said, "Is it Mr. Crawley?" "Yes," she said, "let him be burnt-to the devil with him!"

James Corless, provision dealer, 277, Crown-street, on Saturday, the 13th instant, from ten o'clock to a quarter past ten at night, I heard a loud and pitiful moan, or cry. I looked, and perceived a man running from Lonsdale-street towards Crown-street. I saw a terrific flame issuing from his sides and back, and over his head. It was all over him, but issued from his sides. By the appearance of the flame I thought it was a spirit of some description. I then rushed forth and pulled my coat off. As he got into Crown street be stumbled on his face. I immediately threw the coat over him. There was still a little flame issuing from his head. Another man came up, and we extinguished the flame. The coat was burnt. His moaning ceased when he found he had help. He said nothing, and the police coming up they took him into charge. I felt very nervous and went away. As regards the woman, she has been in the habit of dealing at my shop. She told me that her husband was in a consumption and used to get meat suitable to his complaint.

William Walls, police-officer 233, stated- "I was on duty on the night mentioned in Lonsdale-street. I met deceased at the top of Lonsdale-street, I saw deceased burning, and the last witness put the fire out. When I saw him first he was on the ground, and the last witness and another man were standing over him. I assisted in putting the flames out. I took deceased to the Royal Infirmary in a car. I then came back and apprehended the prisoner, who was in her own house. She was sober. I charged her with throwing oil on her husband.

She said- "He struck me with his fist. He threw a plate and struck me at the back of my head and pulled my hair. I am not sorry for having thrown the oil upon him." She was a little excited but not much. Prisoner here told- "The officer has told a lie. I never said I was not sorry. I have a large lump on my forehead, the result of one of his blows." The witness further produced the clothes the deceased had on at the time.

Detective officer Marsden: "On Monday, the 15th instant, I went to the house No. 1, Lonsdale-street. On going into the kitchen I saw a quantity of paraffin oil had been spilled on the hearth and on the oven, and splashed all over the mantlepiece. I found a number of pieces of bottle lying under the fire grate and on the floor. I produce the largest piece. (This was the neck of a salad oil bottle) It has contained paraffin oil. The oil can be detected by the smell. This piece was on the floor directly opposite the fireplace".

Dr. George Hunt Orton, house surgeon at the Royal Infirmary deposed as follows:- The deceased was brought to the Infirmary on the night of the 13th instant, by Police-officer 233, suffering from severe burns. I examined him and found that the whole of his head and face was charred. His left arm was burned all over, from the fingers to the shoulder. His right hand and forearm were also burnt in the same manner, and also the upper part of his back. Deceased was admitted to the hospital, where he remained until his death, which took place on the 21st instant. Deceased died from the immediate effects of lockjaw, caused by the burns he received. He died at half-past two on Sunday afternoon, rather suddenly".

Mr. Raffles:-" I heard Detective-officer Marsden's testimony. If a portion of the oil went into the fire when the bottle was thrown, the flame might come back and ignite the clothes of the deceased". The prisoner having been duly cautioned, was asked if she had anything to say. She said, "I have nothing to say but what I said before. I am very sorry, but I never threw the oil to burn him. I know nothing of how it caught fire." The prisoner was then committed for trial at the assizes.

THE INQUEST Upon the deceased was also held the same morning before Mr. Clarke Aspinall, the borough coroner. The same evidence was given, and a verdict of "Manslaughter" was returned against the prisoner.

The Crowley 'man on fire' case gives us a valuable insight into Detective Marsden's methods when analysing the scene of a crime. He describes the location of the killing, the layout of the room and the distribution of the paraffin oil. This allows the court to conclude that the bottle had been intentionally thrown and not accidentally spilt by the prisoner. It is also worth noting that the location of the incident (Lonsdale, Almond and Crown Streets) are not in Detective Marsden's usual North Division area of Liverpool. These are streets in the South Division and he may have been brought in to investigate due to his experience as a detective.

THE BIRMINGHAM DAILY POST
1st April 1869

SHOCKING DEATH OF A DRUNKEN HUSBAND. -At the Liverpool Assizes, yesterday Mary Ann Crowley was indicted for causing the death of her husband, by throwing over him a quantity of paraffin oil. The husband had come home drunk and had abused his wife by striking her on the head with his fist. There was a bottle of paraffin oil on the table, and in her momentary rage and vexation she seized it and threw it over him. By some means the oil caught fire, and he was so dreadfully burned that he died in about a week afterwards. The jury found the prisoner guilty but recommended her to mercy on account of the provocation she had received. She was sentenced to one day's imprisonment.

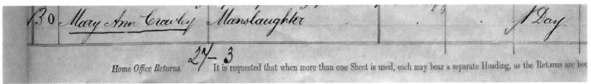

Lancaster Assizes Criminal Register 1869: Mary Ann Crowley sentenced to one day's imprisonment for the manslaughter of her husband.

Similar to the Robert Reid case of 1866, the outcome of this trial illustrates how criminal courts would often take into account the victim's state of intoxication and past relationship with alcohol when considering a sentence. Mary Ann Crowley was seen to be acting in self-defence against a husband who was intoxicated and violent at the time of his killing. It was decided that the throwing of a bottle containing paraffin oil was an act of provocation and even self-defence on her part. After her husband had assaulted her, she grabbed the first item to come to hand - and pre-meditation was therefore ruled out. The circumstances of Michael Crowley's killing became known as the famous 'man on fire' case. The horrifying manner of his death – both for him and those who witnessed it, is still shocking. It forms a chapter in Daniel Longman's (2016) book *Liverpool Macabre Miscellany* which gives a history of Liverpool's most bizarre and disturbing crimes.

Fever Amongst the Liverpool Detectives

During the final week of Mary Ann Crawley's trial (she was sentenced on 30th March 1869), Robert Marsden contracted typhoid fever. This would have almost certainly have been the result of drinking water contaminated with the bacteria *Salmonella Typhii* either at the Police Court on Dale Street, or at the Central Police Office next door. This can be said with a certain degree of confidence as a number of other detectives and court officials (including the magistrate Thomas Raffles) contracted typhoid at the same time. In addition, it appears that no member of Robert's family developed the condition and therefore he did not contract the disease from his home water supply. The source of the bacteria will therefore have been water contaminated with sewerage seeping into drinking water supplied to Police Office and court buildings.

Typhoid Fever

Typhoid fever is divided into four distinct stages, each lasting about a week. In the first week of his illness (approximately 30th March to 5th April) Robert's temperature would have slowly risen and fever fluctuations may have occurred with bradycardia (slow heartbeat), malaise (exhaustion), headache, and cough. He may have suffered from nosebleeds (these are seen in a quarter of cases) and abdominal pain.

From 5th April to 12th April (the second week) Robert will have found that he was too tired to get out of bed. Delirium will have been frequent, often calm, but sometimes agitated. This delirium gives typhoid the nickname of the "nervous fever". A rash known as 'rose spots' will have appeared on Robert's lower chest and abdomen. Diarrhoea may have occurred for him in this stage characterised by its 'typhoid' smell. This gave rise to the belief that typhoid was spread by miasma or 'bad air'. In fact, in a report by the *Liverpool Mercury* on 28th April the 'foul atmosphere of [police] the court' was blamed for this particular typhoid outbreak.

By the third week of his illness (13th April to 20th April), a number of complications could have set in. The first would be intestinal haemorrhage due to bleeding from prolonged diarrhoea. If intestinal perforation had occurred this would have caused septicaemia (blood poisoning) or peritonitis (infection of abdominal cavity). In the fourth week (21st April to 24th April), encephalitis (brain inflammation) would have occurred. Pneumonia and acute bronchitis are common in week four. Neuropsychiatric symptoms (described as "muttering delirium"), with picking at bedclothes or imaginary objects may have been seen. He will have then slipped into unconsciousness and coma. On the morning of 24th April 1869 Robert Marsden died at his home on 30 Fairy Street, Everton. He was 39 years old.

THE LIVERPOOL DAILY POST
26th April 1869

FEVER AMONGST THE DETECTIVES OF LIVERPOOL.— Deaths of Two Officers.— On Saturday the authorities the Central Police Office, Dale-street, received information of the death of Detective Nelson Lees, who expired at four o'clock that morning, after suffering for a few days from typhus fever. He had latterly discharged the duties of crier the court in which Mr. Raffles, the stipendiary magistrate, presides. Some hours later it was made known at the Office that another officer of the force, Robert Marsden, had died that morning, and, as it was understood, of the same disorder. He, too, had been ill but few days. The deceased were the prime of life, were very active, intelligent officers, and had been attached to the police force for many years. It seems that fever has been prevalent amongst the detectives of late. Two of them are now afflicted with it, and one said to be in a very precarious state.

THE LIVERPOOL MERCURY
26th April 1869
DEATH OF TWO LIVERPOOL DETECTIVE OFFICERS–Robert Marsden and Nelson Lees, two old and respected members of the Liverpool detective force, died on Saturday, after a few days illness, of typhus fever. Both men were useful and energetic officers, and during their long period of service had frequently been employed in important cases. Marsden leaves a widow and ten children – all of whom are unable to provide for themselves – and Lees a widow and six children to deplore their loss.

Nurse Emma Thompson was present at his death. It is significant that Emma, rather than Robert's wife Elizabeth, is the informant who registers his death at West Derby Registry Office, Liverpool on 26th April. However, it must be remembered that Elizabeth at this time was pregnant with their tenth child and had a family of young children to look after; she may simply have been in shock. It is tragic that today Robert's condition would be very effectively treated with modern antibiotics. Instead, his painful death shows how precarious life was 150 years ago, and demonstrates how one mouthful of contaminated water could lead to the death of a man in his prime and devastation for his family.

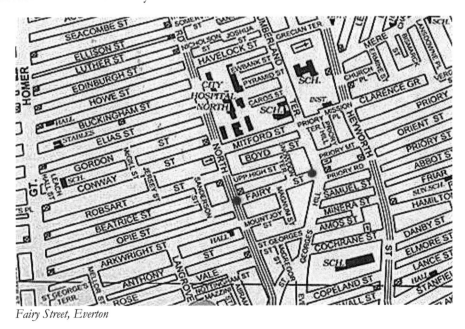

Fairy Street, Everton

Fairy Street where Robert Marsden died of typhoid fever in April 1869. These pictures were taken before the street was demolished in the 1960s. Pictures courtesy of www.losttribeofeverton.com.

Fairy Street no longer exists and is now buried under the grass and trees of Everton Park (see page 14).

Robert Marsden was buried at Anfield Municipal Cemetery, Priory Road, Liverpool on 26th April 1869. He was buried in grave 736 in the Church of England section of the graveyard. Robert was buried in a 'public' grave meaning that a private burial plot was not purchased for him. Public graves were also known as 'paupers' graves and burials were made without a headstone or official grave marker. This may seem curious when taking into account that Robert had been an officer serving in the Liverpool City Police force for at least ten years and was highly respected by both his colleagues and the public. However, it must be remembered that with Robert's passing, his wife Elizabeth and their nine (soon to be ten) children had not only lost their husband and father, but also their main breadwinner and only source of income. To add to this catastrophe, his family were not eligible to receive his police pension on the grounds that he had not served the minimum twenty-five years to make this possible. His family therefore now faced a future of poverty and uncertainty. Any money that his wife Elizabeth immediately possessed would be needed to support her large family, meaning that the purchase of a headstone and a private burial plot would simply have been too great an expense.

Inquiry

Over the weeks and months which followed the typhoid fever outbreak at the Liverpool Central Police Office a number of enquiries were made as to its cause. Mr Raffles the stipendiary magistrate had caught the disease at the same time as Detective Marsden, but he had remarkably recovered. Questions were asked about why a disease, more related to unsanitary buildings and an unhygienic water supply, could have occurred in these newly-built premises which had been constructed at great expense to the town.

The Bradford Daily Telegraph
27th April 1869

AN UNHEALTHY POLICE COURT.

It is only a few years ago that the Liverpool Corporation spent a large sum of money in erecting the Police Courts in Dale Street, and ever since the wretched accommodation for those whom business compelled to attend, and the imperfect ventilation of the principal courts, have been the subject of constant complaints. Even when the courts are only partially filled, the atmosphere is most unwholesome, in proof of which we may cite the following facts:—Mr. Raffles, the stipendiary magistrate, has been for some time, and is now, so ill that he is quite unable to attend to his duties. On Saturday last the crier of the court and a detective officer died, after a very short illness of typhus fever. Three other detectives are also ill with fever, one of them not being expected to recover. The door-keeper also died of typhus a few days ago; and more than one reporter attending there daily is now very seriously indisposed. In the opinion of medical men this fatality is mostly attributable to breathing the poisonous atmosphere.

At the time of the typhoid outbreak the Police Office and Court on Dale Street were less than four years old. However, since their opening these buildings had been the subject of a series of complaints about their poor sanitation and a lack of ventilation. In 1868 Shimmin had already remarked that at the Police Court:

"within the last two years no less than four luckless police officers, all comparatively young and healthy men, who were placed as doorkeepers in [the] lobby, were swept away by frightful fevers, caught here in the discharge of their duties."

He expressed surprise that an outbreak of 'plague' had not already occurred amongst the crowds packed into the lobby and reception areas. He also complained about the lack of ventilation in the building (Chapter 2).

THE LIVERPOOL MERCURY
28th April 1869

THE FOUL ATMOSPHERE OF THE POLICE COURT. At the borough police court yesterday morning, while Messrs. Samuelson and Whitley were sitting. Mr. Lamport entered the court, and asked Detective Inspector Horne what his opinion was as to the cause of the deaths of Detective-officers Marsden and Lees.

In one of the daily papers their deaths had been attributed to the impure atmosphere of the court. Inspector Horne said that both men died from typhus fever. In the case of Marsden it could not be said that he suffered from the impure air of the court, as Marsden was seldom there. Lees' daily duty was inside the court. Mr. Samuelson said that they, as lay magistrates, could bear witness to the fact of the impurity of the atmosphere of the court. Although they were only there occasionally, Mr Raffles as, the stipendiary magistrate, was seriously indisposed, and it was alleged that medical men attributed his (Mr Raffles) loss of health to sitting in that court.

The question had been mooted in the town council two or three times, and the surveyor and architect had had the matter in hand; but still the court was not improved. He should suggest that the court be adjourned to St. George's Hall, or some is other convenient place, while the court was in is its present state.

One of the reporters called attention to the fact that on the last occasion when Marsden attended the court he complained of the stench which came up from the passage by which the prisoners entered the court. Mr. Thornley, solicitor, said several other gentlemen spoke to the disagreeable nature of the odour from the place in question.

Mr. Lamport was of opinion that the impure air of the court arose not so much from the bad ventilation of the court itself as from the fact that there was no ventilation for the cells below except through the court. Mr. Whitley thought the subject should be brought before the town council, and the magistrates concurred in requesting Mr Ellis magistrates' clerk, to make a communication to the Mayor on the subject.

1939 illustration showing various ways that typhoid bacteria can contaminate drinking water.

DEATH'S DISPENSARY.
OPEN TO THE POOR, GRATIS, BY PERMISSION OF THE PARISH.

The theory of 'foul atmosphere', 'bad air' or 'miasma' as the cause of illness was very much at the heart of nineteenth century medicine. By 1869, science had already demonstrated how a contaminated water supply resulted in diseases such as cholera (pictured). However, diseases such as typhoid were thought to be caused by 'impure air' rather than water-borne microbes. In the case of the Police Office and Court on Dale Street, these two buildings were located next to each other and, as stated in the *Bradford Daily Telegraph* of 27th April 1869, were only four years old. Since their completion however, they had been subject to constant problems, not just with ventilation, but a lack of adequate drainage and sanitation for the prisoner cells underneath the court. Perhaps raw sewerage from the prisoners' cells (the smell about which Detective Marsden had recently complained) had been seeping into the drinking water supply of the Police Office?

The Marsden-Lees Subscription Fund is Established.

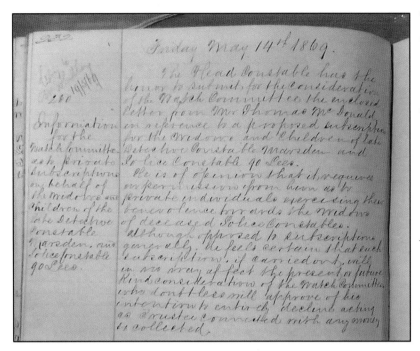

Transcription: *Friday 14th May 1869. The Head Constable has the honor to submit for the consideration of the Watch Committee the enclosed letter from Mr Thomas McDonald in reference to a proposed subscription for the widows and children of late Detective Constable Marsden and Police Constable No.90 Lees. He is of the opinion that it requires no permissions from him as to private individuals exercising their benevolence towards the widows of the deceased Police Constables. Although opposed to subscriptions generally, he feels certain that such subscription, if carried out will in no way affect the present or future kind consideration of the Watch Committee who doubtless will approve of his intention to entirely decline acting as Trustee connected with any money as collected.* (Minutes of the Head Constable to the Liverpool Watch Committee 1969. Liverpool Record Office, Liverpool Libraries)

THE DAILY POST
27th November 1869

THE LATE DETECTIVE OFFICERS MARSDEN AND LEES.— The treasurer acknowledges the following further subscriptions received for the widows and orphans of Detectives Marsden and Lees (per Mr. Campbell):—Mr. James Sykes, 10s; A Friend, 5s; A Friend, 10s; Mr. E. Wilders, 10s; A Friend, 5s; A Private Friend, 5s; Mr. H. Curwen, 5s; Mr. H. A. Abbinett, 10s; Messrs, Byford and Son, 5s; Mr. John Cobb, £1 1s; Mr. James Clegg, £1 1s; Mr. Robert Cain, £1 1s; Messrs. Woodhouse and Co., £1 1s; Mr. Peter Walker, £1 1s; Liverpool Printing Company, £1 1s; Messrs. Albion and Myers, 10s; H. Segar and Co., £1 1s; Messrs. Sykes, Porter, and Co., £1 1s; Messrs. Gardner, Pedder, and Co., £1 1s; Mr. Wm. Clarkson, £1 1s; Copeland and Green, 10s 6d; Mr. Thornley, 10s 6d; Mr. W. W. Matheson, £1 1s; Mr. J. Tarbuck, 10s; Mr. J. Brown, 5s; Mr. Thomas Lamb. 5s.

In May 1869 the 'Marsden-Lees Subscription Fund' was established and the Secretary of Lime Street Station, J Gerrard, volunteered to act as Treasurer. Over the following months the *Liverpool Mercury* and *Daily Post* regularly reported on the progress of the subscription fund, listing the number and value of donations as they accumulated.

Detective Marsden's Widow and Children

Although money from the Marsden-Lees subscription fund would have helped her in the short-term, Elizabeth Marsden still had to find some means of long-term financial support for her children. As she was not eligible to receive Robert's police pension, Elizabeth applied to the Police Superannuation fund for financial aid. She received a weekly stipend of 10 shillings. Less than two years after her husband's death in January 1871, she again appeared before the police Finance, Clothing and Superannuation Fund Sub-Committee. The Committee now reduced her allowance to 8 shillings per week. With a family of nine children, Elizabeth would have found this amount impossible on which to house, clothe and feed her family. Constable Nelson Lees' widow Matilda also appeared before the Sub Committee and saw a reduction in her stipend from 7 shillings per week to 6 shillings.

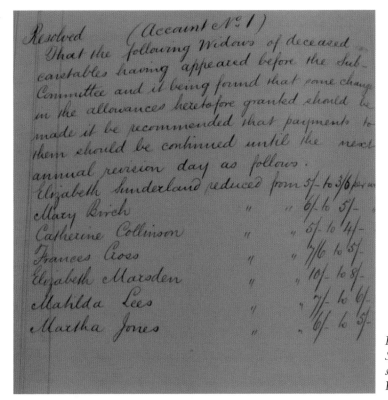

Elizabeth Marsden appears before the Police Superannuation Committee in 1871. Her weekly stipend is reduced to 8 shillings. (Liverpool Records Office)

1871 Census

Within two years of Robert's death, his family had left their home in Fairy Street and moved to 61 Priory Street, Everton. His widow Elizabeth is now aged 41. His eldest daughter Elizabeth (Ann) is aged 20 and is working a machinist. His sons Edward (aged 19, a sailor), William (17, a cab driver) and Robert (16, a sailmaker) are also still living at home. The younger children Harriet (my great, great grandmother, aged 11) and twins Emily and Albert (aged 7) are at school. His son John died aged 4 in January 1870 and is buried close to Robert in Anfield Cemetery (also in an unmarked grave). Henry the baby is now aged 3.

1881 Census

By 1881 all but two of Elizabeth's children have married and moved to their own homes. Elizabeth and her sons Albert (18, a chemical labourer) and Henry (13, at school) are again living back in

Fairy Street (No 39). However, their financial situation is still poor. They are now lodgers of the Wilson family and share the house with ten other people. Elizabeth is working as a charwoman.

1891 Census

Ten years later in 1891 Elizabeth Marsden is now aged 61 and is working as an office cleaner. She lives at 24 Upper High Street, Everton. Her daughter Harried (my great, great grandmother) is married to a William Murray. They, with their nine children (including my great grandmother Maria, aged 10), are Eliza's lodgers.

No record can be found of Elizabeth Marsden in the 1901 census.

Elizabeth died in 1907 at the age of 79 at her home in Upper High Street, Everton. She survived her husband Robert by almost forty years. It is a testimony to her resilience that she managed to raise their eight surviving children completely on her own by working as a charwoman and office cleaner. Elizabeth is buried (again in an unmarked grave) in Kirkdale Cemetery, Longmoor Lane, Liverpool.

Court, Saltney Street. © Liverpool Records Office, Liverpool Libraries.

Legacy

Robert Marsden's life as a detective in Liverpool City Police Force gives us an absorbing glimpse of Victorian Liverpool (in all its different guises) and illustrates how the personality of the city was shaped by the people who came to it over the centuries. It is said that the people of Liverpool have a tough and unique character. This character has been moulded by the vast array of cultures and influences brought to it through its bonds with the sea. In the nineteenth century, the brutality of the African slave trade and the cruelty of the men who manned Liverpool's slave ships had left its mark. Those who had lived through the starvation and horror of the Irish potato famine and those who lived the brutal existence of life on board ship; the barbarous privateers and whalers; and those born into the desperate grinding poverty of slum housing in industrial Britain. All influenced and shaped the character of the city.

How did Robert Marsden view the people he worked amongst? How did he return home each night to his wife and eight children after long hours tramping the dark and dangerous streets, courts and alleyways investigating theft, violence and murder? Was he equally hardened and brutalised? It is very probable that he was. But we can also see from his involvement in the rescue of street children that there was a benevolent side to his character. He understood the advantages of taking children out of the poverty which created and drove criminal behaviour. He saw that lives could be saved and that future criminals could be removed from the streets.

Robert Marsden's early death at the age of thirty-nine was a disaster for his family. His widow Elizabeth never re-married, and as we follow her and their children through the censuses of 1871, 1881 and 1891, we can see their poverty increasing. Living as lodgers in cramped boarding houses with other families, Elizabeth worked as a charwoman and office cleaner in order to support her younger children. The ever-present danger of poverty and destitution faced by many families after the loss of their only breadwinner had become a painful reality for Elizabeth. Robert's loss certainly changed the course of his children's lives and as a consequence, those of his descendants.

His untimely death was also a tragedy for the town of Liverpool and its police force. Newspaper reports describe him as 'one of the finest and most able detectives'. He was called an officer of great intelligence and integrity, admired even by Hugh Shimmin, who was one of Liverpool City Police Force's most out-spoken critics at that time. The unprecedented step of creating a relief fund for his widow and children demonstrates the esteem in which Robert was held by the people of the town. If he had lived, he may have achieved much more.

For the last hundred and fifty years, Robert Marsden has laid forgotten in an unmarked grave in Anfield Cemetery. My hope is that this biography acts as a long-delayed memorial to his memory. It is my aim that any royalties received for this book will contribute to a fitting headstone, which will mark the final resting place of Robert Marsden - a most intelligent detective officer of Liverpool City Police Force.

EPILOGUE

Scotland Road at three o'clock in the morning was never a cheerful prospect. Even in the summer, its soot-blackened buildings and cobbled roadway had a desolate look. On this bleak November night it looked positively brutal. A storm roared across the Irish Sea, picking up momentum as it screamed and howled through the rigging of ships straining at their moorings in the docks and river. The wind and rain hurled itself into the faces of Detectives Marsden and Fitzsimmons as they marched south towards Dale Street and the Liverpool Central Police Office.

Marsden, water pouring from the brim of his leather top-hat squinted briefly into the streaming darkness. He was a tall slender man, with pleasantly blunt features and shrewd green eyes. His brown hair and whiskers were plastered to his forehead and cheeks. He turned to Fitzsimmons and shouted above the roar of the wind. "The beat constable should be here by now!". The sharp beating of a wooden stick on the pavement somewhere ahead caused the two officers to stop. "That's him now..." Fitzsimmons replied. Marsden immediately put two fingers to his mouth and whistled the customary reply to a brother officer calling for assistance.

The stick rapped again, this time accompanied by the sounds of screams and cursing from a crowd of figures which began spill out of Robsart Street ahead. "It sounds like a row brewing, come on" Marsden shouted. Bending their heads into the gale the two officers set off towards the group at a steady trot. The crowd saw them and immediately scattered - magically disappearing into alleyways and entries. Marsden and Fitzsimmons increased their pace to a sprint as they gave chase. Turning the corner, they ran into the pitch-black mouth of Robsart Street. Its darkness instantly swallowed them. Scotland Road returned to the roaring wind and the hissing of the rain on the cobbles.

ACKNOWLEDGMENTS

Many thanks to Mike Pealing for his valuable advice.

REFERENCES

Archer, J E. (2011) *The Monster Evil: Policing and Violence in Victorian Liverpool*. Liverpool: Liverpool University Press.

Archibald, M. (2015) *Liverpool Gangs, Vice and Packet Rats: 19th Century Crime and Punishment*. Edinburgh: Black and White Publishing Ltd.

Bronte, E. (1847) *Wuthering Heights*. New York: Barnes and Noble.

Clarkson, T. (1836) *The History of the Rise, Progress, and Accomplishment of the Abolition of the Slave-Trade*. by the British Parliament.

Cockcroft, WR. (1991) *From Cutlasses to Computers: The Police Force in Liverpool 1836-1989*. Market Drayton: SB Publications.

The Head Constable's Reports to the Liverpool Watch Committee 1860-1869. Liverpool Records Office 352 POL1/1-37

Dickens, C. (1861) 'Poor Mercantile Jack' in *The Uncommercial Traveller*

Longman, DK. (2016) *Liverpool: A Macabre Miscellany*. Stroud: Amberley Publishing.

Macilwee, M. (2011) *The Liverpool Underworld: Crime in the City 1750-1900*. Liverpool: Liverpool University Press.

McLevy, J. (1974) *The Casebook of a Victorian Detective*. Edinburgh: Canongate.

Moss, A. & Skinner, K (2013) *The Victorian Detective*. Oxford: Shire Publications.

Parry, D. (2011) *Murder in Victorian Liverpool*. Lancaster, Palatine Books.

Shimmin, H. (1862) *Liverpool Sketches*. Liverpool

Shimmin, H. (1868) 'The Police Court I-IV'. *The Porcupine*. 7 November-12 December 1868.

Shimmin, H. (1870) 'Bridewell Sketches I-IV'. *The Porcupine*. 12 November-10 December 1870

Shpayer-Makov, H. (2011) *The Ascent of the Detective: Police Sleuths in Victorian and Edwardian England*. Oxford: Oxford University Press.

Stewart, E J. (2019) *Courts and Alleys: A History of Liverpool Courtyard Housing*. Liverpool: Liverpool University Press.

Wade, S. (2007) *Plain Clothes & Sleuths: A History of Detectives in Britain*. Stroud: Tempus Publishing.

Walton, JK., and Wilcox, A. (1991) *Low Life and Moral Improvement in Mid-Victorian England: Liverpool Through the Journalism of Hugh Shimmin*. Leicester: Leicester University Press.

Boundary Terrace, Liverpool

Steble Fountain, William Brown Street.

Isla Broadwell (@IslaBroadwell)/Twitter

www.islabroadwellbooks.com

islabroadwellbooks@mail.com